REVOLUTIONARY
RUSSIA, 1917

REVOLUTIONARY RUSSIA, 1917

John M. Thompson

AMERICAN UNIVERSITIES FIELD STAFF

CHARLES SCRIBNER'S SONS · NEW YORK

Copyright © 1981 Charles Scribner's Sons

Library of Congress Cataloging in Publication Data

Thompson, John M.
    Revolutionary Russia, 1917.

        Bibliography: p.
        Includes index.
        1.   Soviet Union—History—Revolution, 1917-1921.
I.   Title.
DK265.T54   947.084′1   81-8783
ISBN 0-684-17278-X   AACR2
ISBN 0-684-17277-1 (pbk.)

3 5 7 9 11 13 15 17 19   F/C   20 18 16 14 12 10 8 6 4 2
5 7 9 11 13 15 17 19   F/P   20 18 16 14 12 10 8 6 4 2

Printed in the United States of America

096064

FOR A. F. T.,
who waited patiently for so long

Contents

Introduction

The Russian Revolution of 1917 has profoundly affected the recent history of the world. Its impact has been felt in every corner of the globe. People, ideas, events have all been touched by it. Yet, though knowledge and understanding of the Russian Revolution are crucial to the study of modern literature, politics, and social science, no adequate short history of the revolution exists in English. Soviet historians and ideologues have written copiously on the events and meaning of 1917. Participants have provided vivid and varied accounts from many perspectives. Scholars in Western Europe and the United States have published well-researched and revealing monographs on various aspects of the revolution. But these books are too long, or too partisan, or too specialized to serve the general reader well.

In writing this account I had three goals. First, to provide basic information on the revolution—a short, clear narrative of what happened. Second, to incorporate recent thinking and writing about the events of 1917. During the last ten or fifteen years scholars both inside and outside the Soviet Union have completed significant new research on the revolution, resulting in a dozen or so major books and articles on various aspects of the subject.[1] On a research exchange visit to the Soviet Union in 1969 I talked with a number of Soviet historians of the revolution; I have also kept in touch with Western specialists. Research continues, but this seems an appropriate moment to synthesize recently developed knowledge. I have not, however, adopted all the conclusions recent writers have reached.

My third goal was to go beyond description to analyze what happened and to discuss the "whys" of the revolution. Within the bounds of reasonable speculation, I have raised interpretive questions about the events of 1917 in an effort to stimulate the interest and thinking of students. For too long the history of the Russian Revolution has been treated either dogmatically (by both Marxists and anti-Communists) or cautiously (by Western writers who are aware that data are limited and interpretation is risky). This study deliberately tries to pose some of the major questions that need discussion and further study.

NAMES AND DATES

The terminology of the Russian Revolution is confusing. Some of this confusion, particularly that connected with names and dates, can be cleared up quite easily. That associated with ideology and politics is much harder to clarify.

In the first place, the term "The Russian Revolution" is a misnomer. If we define "revolution" as a radical and fairly sudden change in a political or social system, not one but two revolutions took place in Russia in 1917. The first was a popular revolt against the tsarist government and administration which led to the collapse and disappearance of the tsarist rule that had lasted for 300 years. The calendar used in Russia until February 1, 1918, was the old Julian calendar, which in 1917 was thirteen days behind the

---

[1] See the Guide to Further Reading at the back of the book. For an excellent review of recent Western literature, see Theodore J. Uldricks, "Petrograd Revisited: New Views of the Russian Revolution," *The History Teacher,* 3, no. 4 (August 1975), 611–623.

modern Gregorian calendar. The overthrow of the tsardom in the capital, Petrograd (later Leningrad), occurred on February 24 through 28, 1917, according to the old calendar, and Soviet writers call that uprising the "February Revolution." Under the modern calendar this same revolution happened on March 8 through 12; hence Western writers often refer to it as the "March Revolution."

A related confusion of names applies to the second revolution in 1917. It saw the disintegration of the Provisional government that had formally replaced the tsarist administration in March and the coming to power in Petrograd of a radical Marxist party, the Bolsheviks. This occurred on October 24 and 25, 1917, under the old calendar, and is widely known in Soviet writings as the "October Revolution" (often "the Great October Socialist Revolution"). The same series of events took place on November 6 and 7, 1917, according to the modern calendar, and outside the Soviet Union it is frequently referred to as the "November Revolution."

In a clear permutation of names and dates but in an effort to use both the more commonly accepted terms and the modern calendar, in this book I will call the revolutions the February Revolution and the October Revolution but will give specific dates according to the modern calendar. See Table 1 for more information.

Now we have two revolutions instead of one. But do we? The events known as the February and October revolutions are distinct and definable, to be sure. A clear shift in political power took place in each instance. Yet some have argued that these two "revolutions" were simply incidents in a much broader revolutionary process in Russia. They see what occurred in 1917 as a minor step in a long march toward the modernization of Russian society that lasted from the 1860s until the 1940s.[2] Others treat the revolutions of 1917 as reflections of a widespread disintegration of the Russian social system that began in the 1890s and was halted only by the establishment of totalitarian rule in the 1930s. Thus for many "The Russian Revolution" continues to have greater significance than the more precise appellations, February and

[2] See C. E. Black et al., *The Modernization of Japan and Russia: A Comparative Study* (New York, 1975).

Table 1.   NAMES AND DATES IN THE RUSSIAN REVOLUTIONS OF 1917

The First Revolution: The February or March Revolution

Old-Style Dates		New-Style Dates
February 24	Demonstrations begin in Petrograd	March 8
February 25	Strikes and crowds in streets grow	March 9
February 26	Strikes spread; first clashes with police	March 10
February 27	Tsar orders use of force; firing on demonstrators	March 11
February 28	Soldiers mutiny; government loses control; Petrograd Soviet formed; Duma leaders meet	March 12

The Second Revolution: The October or November Revolution

October 24	Provisional government moves against Bolsheviks in Petrograd; Military Revolutionary Committee of the Soviet prepares defense and for armed uprising	November 6
October 25	Forces of Soviet occupy key points; government loses control; Second Congress of Soviets convenes	November 7
October 26	Ministers of Provisional government arrested; new Soviet government formed by Bolsheviks	November 8

October revolutions. Both aspects of the revolution are important. The chapters that follow will focus on the specific events of 1917, which so changed Russian society and Russia's role in international affairs, but will also discuss the symbolic significance and worldwide influence of "The Russian Revolution" in the decades since 1917.

In defining our subject, years as well as names create problems. When indeed did the Russian Revolution occur? Can we limit our focus to eight months in 1917? What about the long history of the revolutionary movement in Russia before 1917? How can one neglect the shattering period from 1918 to 1921, years of civil war and a Bolshevik-led struggle against foreign intervention? And did not the revolution affect Russian society most profoundly only in 1928–1929 when Joseph V. Stalin became a dictator and decreed the rapid industrialization of the country and the forced collectivization of agriculture? Admittedly someone writing a full history of the Russian Revolution might want to consider all these issues in detail. To keep this account brief, however, the pre-1917 background to the revolution is summarized in Chapter One while the cataclysmic events of 1918–1921 are touched on in the last two chapters.

How accurate is it to speak of "The *Russian* Revolution"? Not very, it seems. The events of 1917 occurred in a multinational empire in which Russians (or more precisely, Great Russians) were only slightly more than half the total population. Other Slavic peoples—Ukrainians and Byelorussians—as well as dozens of other nationalities played important roles in the Russian Revolution. Their nationalist aspirations helped undermine the tsarist administration, weakened the moderate Provisional government that was in power between the February and October revolutions, and created major difficulties for the revolutionary Soviet government set up by the Bolsheviks. Although in this study the customary term "Russian Revolution" will be used, the reader should always keep in mind that many others besides Russians participated in the great upheavals of 1917.

Beyond the complexity of dates and names, the Russian Revolution is a term laden with ideological meanings. Observers frequently see this major occurrence in modern history in the light of their own beliefs and concerns. For some it is the opening of an era of freedom and socialist beneficence for the masses. For others it marks the starting point of a new and all-encompassing tyranny of the state over the individual. For still others it represents a bright future aborted—a promise of social democracy broken, or the development of Russian liberalism sidetracked. These are matters of interpretation rather than definition and cannot be easily resolved. Many of the issues raised by such preconceived

NATIONALITIES IN THE WESTERN HALF OF THE RUSSIAN EMPIRE, 1900

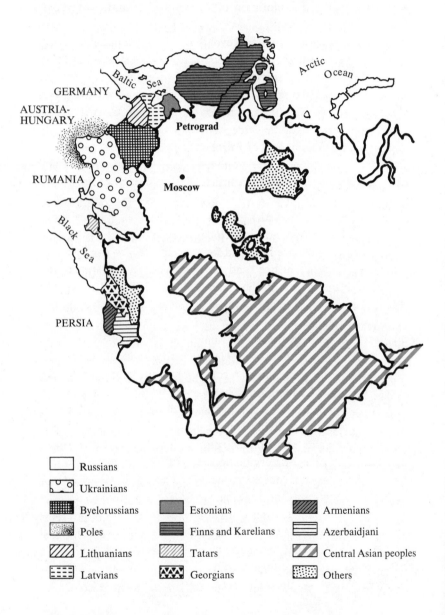

Russians

Ukrainians

Byelorussians

Poles

Lithuanians

Latvians

Estonians

Finns and Karelians

Tatars

Georgians

Armenians

Azerbaidjani

Central Asian peoples

Others

views of the Russian Revolution will be examined later; here it is only appropriate to state my own assumptions so that the reader knows whence the exploration of the revolution that follows has begun.

In my view, the Russian Revolution was a tumultuous event in the modern struggle of the peoples of the Russian Empire to improve their lives. Individuals and groups defined a better life in different ways. To many it meant primarily the ability to control their own affairs, whether as a nation, as an ethnic minority, or as individual citizens. Some were determined that the country not fall under the domination of European powers. Others battled for national independence or autonomy against Russian rulers. Still others fought for the right to participate in government and social affairs.

Other concerns exerted a powerful attraction as well. Millions demanded better food, housing, clothing, and jobs. The rural population pressed for more land and fewer burdens. Many people also insisted on social justice and equality, decent treatment and respect for the rights of the individual and the group, and the opportunity to act freely. Almost everyone wanted peace and security.

Few of these aspirations were fulfilled in 1917. Many are not yet achieved, either in the Soviet Union or elsewhere in the world. But what drove the engine of revolution was the compelling desire of the peoples of Russia for a better life, however each group or individual defined it. Peasants wanted land and to be left alone; workers demanded a living wage and decent conditions; liberals desired civil rights and political participation; nationalities strove for autonomy or self-determination. They could not agree on what the revolution meant, but everyone believed in it. Like the French Revolution before it, the Russian Revolution came to stand for a new order, a better existence for human beings everywhere. It is that dream far more than the growth of Soviet power and influence around the globe that has made the Russian Revolution a driving force in contemporary history and the modern world, from Spain to Vietnam, from Chile to China.

ACKNOWLEDGMENTS

I wish to acknowledge with gratitude support in preparing this study from the Guggenheim Memorial Foundation, the International Research and Exchanges Board, and Indiana University.

I am indebted to those who provided me with library and other facilities: Father Gustav Wetter, Oriental Institute, Rome; E. A. Bayne, Center for Mediterranean Studies of the American Universities Field Staff, Rome; and the librarians, American Academy in Rome. I also wish to thank those Soviet scholars who graciously discussed their work and views on the revolution with me: P. V. Volobuyev, E. N. Burdzhalov, A. L. Fraiman, E. G. Gimpel'son, I. I. Mints, and Iu. S. Tokarev. Finally, I have profited greatly from the critical reading of the draft manuscript and the useful suggestions provided by William G. Rosenberg and Alexander Rabinowitch. As is customary, they are not in the least responsible for my errors and opinions.

REVOLUTIONARY
RUSSIA, 1917

1
Prelude to Revolution

★

RUSSIAN SOCIETY BEFORE 1917

In the half-century before 1917, Russian society was in ferment. Until 1861 Russia had for 300 years been a predominantly agricultural system maintained by the labor and taxes of peasant-serfs. This system had developed in the fifteenth and sixteenth centuries when the princes of Moscow were establishing centralized authority over other territories in European Russia. Taking the title of tsar (or caesar), they expanded their control and fought Germans, Swedes, Poles, Turks, and Tatars in the process. Since land was the primary resource but had little value without people to work it, the tsars distributed land to their warrior nobles and increasingly bound the peasants to the land. Before long the peasant-serf was not free to move at all, and eventually could be sold apart from land (and even family), becoming in essence the slave of the noble. In many areas the serfs were organized in a village commune (called *mir* or *obshchina*) which was collectively responsible for work on the noble's land, for taxes, and for recruits for the tsarist army. Despite minor changes, this system endured and was even extended during the reigns of Peter the Great and Catherine the Great in the eighteenth century.

In the nineteenth century, however, it became increasingly clear that serfdom was anachronistic and inefficient. When England and France handily defeated Russia in the Crimean War (1854–1856), many in Russia, including the new tsar, Alexander II, decided that serfdom should be abolished. After lengthy consultation among nobles and bureaucrats, Alexander decreed the emancipation of the serfs in 1861. But when the serfs were freed, many of them received insufficient land. Moreover, the emancipation legislation placed them under fiscal and social obligations to the village commune, which in turn was responsible to the state. Not only were conditions difficult for many peasants, but they felt that the emancipation had cheated them of their just right to all the land. Thus they became increasingly restive, resenting both the nobles, who still held much of the land, and the government, which they believed had deceived them.

By the early 1900s, the peasants were in desperate straits. High fertility in the preceding decades had increased their numbers, which intensified their land hunger. Dues and taxes were a heavy burden, and famine and epidemics broke out sporadically in peasant regions. At the same time, other groups in Russia were becoming increasingly hostile to the tsarist system and government. Thus Japan's easy defeat of Russia in the Russo-Japanese War of 1904–1905 helped spark an unsuccessful uprising known as the Revolution of 1905. During this upheaval, peasant revolts were widespread and serious, many having to be suppressed by special military units sent into the countryside. As a result, the government reduced the obligations of the peasants and planned basic changes in the structure of agriculture. The major Russian statesman of the time, Count S. I. Witte, formulated this new policy, but it was initiated under his successor as prime minister, P. A. Stolypin. The changes, often referred to as the Stolypin reforms, were designed to dissolve the peasant communes, encourage individual peasant ownership of land, and improve the social and legal status of the peasantry. But Stolypin was assassinated and World War I broke out before the reforms could be fully implemented.

Though it seems probable that completion of the Stolypin reforms would have made peasant society more productive and more stable, little could be done about the runaway growth of the peasant population. There were too many peasant mouths to be fed and too little land for peasants to work. It is estimated that there were some 55 million peasants in 1861, 85 million at the time of the census of 1897, and 115 million in 1913, just before World War I. While the agricultural population more than doubled between 1861 and 1913, the land available to the peasants increased in the same period only about 50 percent. This made the pressure for land—indeed for survival—a crushing dilemma.

Not only was Russia's rural population undergoing rapid change before 1917, but her industry and work force as well were in a period of transition. The Industrial Revolution had swept through most of northwestern Europe during the first half of the nineteenth century, but its full impact was not felt in Russia until the last quarter of that century. Partly in an effort to match the burgeoning power of its European neighbors, partly in hopes of bettering the lives of the Russian peoples, the Russian government actively promoted industrialization from the 1880s onward. Russia's rich natural resources and a plentiful if untrained supply of labor from among the recently emancipated peasants favored rapid industrial growth. Much of the necessary technology and financing came from Western capitalist countries, a feature that the Bolsheviks harped on in 1917. Through a system of taxation and controlled grain exports the government placed much of the cost of industrialization on the already overburdened and disgruntled peasants.

Industrialization in Russia had many of the same effects as elsewhere in the world. Cities grew far too rapidly, workers were crowded together under wretched conditions, and old values and social ties were undercut. Unemployment, discontent, and alienation were common. Russian industrialization, however, had certain special characteristics that contributed to a revolutionary situation. Industrial production was highly concentrated, both in a few major cities and regions—such as Moscow, the Urals, the Ukraine, and St. Petersburg (later Petrograd)—and in particularly large factories, such as the Putilov works, which gathered thousands of workers in one place. Consequently, large agglomerations of workers existed, giving them greater solidarity and facilitating the spread and penetration of revolutionary ideas among them. Moreover, the important role of state and foreign capital, government intervention in and control over economic affairs, and the secondary position of businessmen in a Russian society that was still largely feudal and aristocratic all hindered the emergence of a strong group of Russian capitalists. Since their economic power and numbers were limited, the industrialists could not play as large a political role as they had in Western Europe and the United States. Vladimir Ilich Lenin was undoubtedly correct when he noted that although the Russian workers' movement was weak compared with those in Western Europe, the Russian proletariat was relatively quite strong because of the feebleness of the Russian bourgeoisie.

The general modernization of Russian society that was occurring at this time also helped to create a revolutionary situation. Transportation and communications were improving rapidly, education and literacy more slowly. But the overall effect was to facilitate the movement of people and ideas around Russia. Both the knowledge and the aspirations of the masses increased dramatically, so that appeals for revolutionary change not only reached more people but found among them a readier response.

Moreover, the spread of education and the greater social mobility that accompanied modernization, especially when confronted by the continuing conservatism of Russia's ruling classes, helped produce a well-prepared and alienated revolutionary elite anxious to lead the discontented peasants and workers against the old order. The flux and frustrations of Russian society in the half-century before the revolution made it a natural breeding ground for revolutionaries. A volatile combination soon existed: exploited workers, desperate peasants, and angry intellectuals. Only an ideology and an unbending government were needed to set off the explosion. The tsarist system supplied the latter and Karl Marx the former.

IDEAS

Science, technology, and education are key factors in the process of modernization in any society. They create new ideas and undermine old values. In the Russian case the intellectual assault on the old order was particularly overwhelming because the premodern belief system was already weak and brittle.

The norms that had held Russian society together in the past were obedience to an autocratic but benign tsar, the rituals and vague "togetherness" provided by Orthodox Christianity, a class system of obligations and service to the state, and a mystical belief in the uniqueness (and goodness) of Slavic peasant tradition. By the early twentieth century all of these had become vitiated or outmoded. Educated Russians of all classes found the autocratic essence of tsarist power increasingly oppressive and antiquated, and even the peasants, longtime believers in the goodness of the "Father-Tsar," found it hard to maintain that faith in the face of the tsar's obvious inability or unwillingness to do anything to relieve their plight. Most of the bishops and priests of the Orthodox Church, while undoubtedly providing comfort and reassurance to many, opposed social activism and offered little to help people cope with the changing times. Individuals and groups were increasingly asserting their own rights over those of the state or the collective whole, and neither peasantism nor Slavic tradition seemed an answer to the complexities of modern life. Moreover, no new conservative or stabilizing values emerged to replace those that were withering away. This helps to explain why the old order collapsed so rapidly and disappeared almost completely in 1917.

Nevertheless, there were lots of new ideas in prerevolutionary Russia. Most of them came from the West, in a process of infiltration that had begun in the sixteenth and seventeenth centuries and still continues today. Russians had been agonizing for hundreds of years over how best to cope with values and precepts received from the West. Counsels of rejection, of adaptation, and of imitation were plentiful. In the nineteenth century, partly as a result of the spread of university education, a group of intellectuals emerged who were anxious to change Russia, in one way or another, the majority of whom opposed the tsarist regime. These revolutionaries seldom came from the peasantry but were most often offspring of various middle classes, including bureaucrats, priests, and merchants, though a few were of noble origin. They struggled to apply the principles of the Enlightenment, of German idealist philosophy, and of European socialism and anarchism to Russian conditions. Guilt and frustration were often the chief results. They suffered over the glaring discrepancy between the reality of Russian life and the values of modern Western society, and they felt scorned by the government, which seemed consistently to block their every effort to improve conditions and reform the system.

Until the twentieth century the revolutionaries were cut off not only from the government but also from the great mass of the people. The peasants, not understanding who the revolutionaries were or what they were saying, rejected them. The workers and artisans resented and distrusted the privileged classes, from which most revolutionaries sprang. But after 1900 the new ideas from the West, the revolutionary elites, and the disgruntled masses began to coalesce in a combustible mixture that ignited explosively in 1917. Three main currents of Western thought were involved: liberalism, socialism, and nationalism.

The revolutionaries who espoused Western liberalism believed that the salvation of Russia lay in its continued industrialization and modernization. Key elements of the new order they favored were fully protected civil liberties, representative government, and a constitutional system.

The two most important schools of socialist thought were Marxism and peasant socialism. For Marxists the goal was an industrialized and socialist society. But first Russia had to go through a capitalist stage of development, and for this to occur a so-called bourgeois-democratic revolution to overthrow the feudal-bureaucratic tsarist government was needed. After that the growing proletariat could be mobilized to undertake a socialist revolution. The revolutionary Marxists were organized in the Russian Social Democratic Labor Party (RSDLP). Their main socialist opponents were found in the Socialist Revolutionary Party. Its leaders believed that Russia could achieve socialism without fully passing through industrial capitalism. Instead, the Socialist Revolutionaries (or SRs) maintained, once the tsarist system was overthrown, the socialization of agriculture—collective ownership of and production on the land—would lead smoothly to a fully socialized society in which both industry and agriculture would be managed to meet the needs of the whole population.

Nationalism was an idea that cut two ways. For some it meant the greater power and glory of the centralized Russian state, both against non-Russians within the Russian Empire and against European and Asian powers outside. But for non-Russians it meant the assertion of their cultural identity and social and political autonomy against the centralized authority of the Russian government.

SOCIAL AND POLITICAL FACTORS

Nationalism had clear-cut and direct political repercussions. Its impact on the Russian leaders and public helped involve Russia in World War I, even though some farsighted observers predicted that Russian society was too weak and unstable to withstand the stress of a major conflict. Nationalism also led to agitation by non-Russians, particularly Poles, Finns, Ukrainians, and Baltic peoples, for autonomy or independence for their regions.

Other aspects of prerevolutionary politics in Russia reflected rapid change and basic instability. Under the pressure of the Revolution of 1905, Tsar Nicholas II had grudgingly made certain concessions which had helped the government to weather the storm. Among these were some civil liberties for the population and creation of a limited system of representative government in the form of an indirectly elected legislative body, the Duma. From 1907 to 1917 Russian citizens enjoyed greater basic freedoms than they had ever had before, and the Duma worked quite well. But these halting steps toward a democratic political system were undercut by the basic mistrust among all those involved. Politically aware citizens and the liberal politicians of the Duma had no faith in the tsarist government and administration, while the tsar, his advisers, and many government officials deeply resented the new system and its supporters.

This political abyss of mutual suspicion and distrust was complemented by deep class divisions in Russian society as a whole. Not only did much of the educated public detest "them"—the court circles and the government—but the great mass of workers and peasants were increasingly hostile to and alienated from all the propertied and educated classes above them. As their expectations rose, the lower classes believed they were being deprived of basic justice and of a fair share of the social good. They felt powerless to control their own affairs and more and more desperate over the conditions in which they lived. This growing gulf between the masses and the elite in Russian society may well have been unbridgeable.

Finally, a crucial political factor in the prerevolutionary situation was the rigid and unyielding nature of the tsarist system itself. One difficulty was that many senior officials, and probably Tsar Nicholas II himself, continued to believe in the undiluted autocratic power of the tsar despite the reforms that followed the Revolution of 1905. They took literally Part I of the Fundamental Laws of the Russian Empire, which stated: "The All-Russian Emperor possesses Supreme and Autocratic power. To obey His authority not only from fear but also from conscience is ordered by God Himself." This meant that their fundamental position was to resist change, to be uncompromising even on minor points. In a time of stress and crisis, this was suicidal.

Moreover, the bureaucratic system was structured to oppose change. The leading officials had ordinarily achieved their posts by adhering strictly to traditional regulations and old ways of doing things. There was little incentive to innovate or to make imaginative departures in policy. There was no established mechanism for within-system change. This meant that only occasional power-ful personalities, such as Witte and Stolypin, could develop new approaches. Although neither man was in the least radical, both recognized that certain aspects of Russian society had to be mod-ernized. Yet Witte was defeated in 1906 by the personal opposi-tion of the tsar and some leading conservatives, and Stolypin was assassinated in 1911. After that no strong, reform-minded indi-vidual appeared inside the government. There was no further opportunity for the system to modify itself before it was blown away by the revolutionary storm of 1917.

This discussion of the nature of prerevolutionary Russian society has emphasized certain features that put in question the stability and capacity for change of that society. There were, however, many trends that favored an orderly, peaceful development of Russian society. Among them were the continued rapid growth of the economy, the dramatic and widespread increase in credit, the rise of producers' and consumers' cooperatives, the gradual implementation of the Stolypin reforms, the spread of primary and secondary education, the beginnings of an intellectual and social renaissance among a few Orthodox religious thinkers, and the increasing sophistication and effectiveness of politicians and indus-trialists outside the government. All these factors favored the non-violent evolution of Russian society, but they needed time to make their impact felt. This time was not vouchsafed them.

WHAT BROUGHT ON THE REVOLUTION?

The simplest answer to the question of what actually brought the revolution about is Russia's disastrous involvement in World War I. This cut short the evolutionary developments just men-tioned and greatly intensified four important trends that proved to be the immediate causes of the collapse of the tsarist system in the February Revolution. Among these, three were also sig-nificant factors aiding the Bolsheviks' rise to power in the October Revolution: the disorientation of Russian society, the people's sense of injustice, and the collapse of the economy. Only the fourth factor—the discrediting of the tsar—was eliminated by the February Revolution.

First, the war accelerated the disorientation of Russian society that the processes of modernization, industrialization, and urbanization had launched in the preceding decades. Millions of Russians were physically displaced, some 15 million men by mobilization into the army, millions more as refugees from the war zone or to undertake war work in factories, on farms, and in various war-related organizations. This great migration of individuals within the country meant that old ties, habits, and attitudes were disrupted and that people were exposed to new ideas and experiences. The result was to weaken the fabric of the old society greatly, to leave many people and groups searching for new roots, and to facilitate the process of radical social and political change.

A second trend the war intensified was the sense of injustice and resentment that had been building among the Russian masses in the previous decades. Although at first there was a surge of patriotic support for the war, people became both exhausted and bitter as the war dragged on. Russian losses in the war were overwhelming: almost six million soldiers killed, wounded, and captured; millions of civilians displaced to become refugees in inner Russia; almost one-quarter of the richest lands of the empire lost to the enemy. Many families suffered personally and directly; everyone was affected indirectly. And it all seemed so unfair and hopeless.

Struggling to continue agricultural production after many able-bodied men had been drafted into the army, peasant families found prices of manufactured goods they needed rising faster than prices at which they could sell their grain. Because of the incompetence of the government and the ineptness of many officers, soldiers at the front were often poorly equipped and badly led. Their sacrifices seemed to them pointless, and no matter how stoically they endured or how bravely they fought, they continued to be subjected—in the tradition of the tsarist army—to harsh and arbitrary discipline and were customarily treated as inferior beings. As Allan Wildman concludes, "The soldiers felt they were being used and recklessly expended by the rich and powerful, of whom their officers were the most visible, immediate representatives."[1] War-weariness, despair, and hatred of the old system became dominant throughout all levels of Russian society. The people's only hope seemed to lie in victory—which seemed increasingly illusory—or in a radical change, some sudden liberation from their bonds and burdens.

The third and most immediate cause of the revolution was the partial breakdown of the Russian economy under the strain of war and the resultant deterioration of conditions in the major cities. Prices rose faster than workers' wages. Moreover, as noted earlier, the price structure for the exchange of manufactured and agricultural goods became more and more unfavorable for the peasants. Many, therefore, began to withhold grain and produce from the market. At the same time, the transportation and distribution systems, overburdened by the war, ceased to function effectively for civilian needs. Because of these factors, food and fuel shortages occurred in the cities and living conditions worsened. The misery of urban and barracks life led directly to the disorders which brought down the tsarist government in the late winter of 1917.

The fourth factor—and the only one the February Revolution actually altered—was the institution of the tsardom under Nicholas II. Russia's participation in the war completely discredited his already weak regime. Almost from its inception tsarism had had its detractors and opponents within Russia. During the nineteenth century those who abhorred the injustice and arbitrariness of autocratic tsarist rule became liberal critics, revolutionaries, terrorists, and exiles, but their numbers remained small. The bulk of the population continued to believe in the divinely inspired guardianship of the tsar. In the years immediately preceding the revolution this blind faith began to dissipate. On the one hand, the spread of education and the dissemination of modern views of governance weakened the belief of the people in the somewhat mystical principle of an autocratic tsar. On the other hand, the actions (and

[1] Allan K. Wildman, *The End of the Russian Imperial Army: The Old Army and the Soldiers' Revolt, March–April 1917* (Princeton, 1979), p. 89.

inaction) of the last tsar, Nicholas II, served directly to undermine popular adherence to the system he symbolized.

Nicholas II was definitely the wrong man in the wrong place at
the wrong time. Whether the course of events in Russia in the
twentieth century would have been different if the tsar at that time
had been strong-willed and decisive, knowledgeable and farsighted, is pure speculation. But it is clear that Nicholas's character
and abilities were as poorly suited as was possible to the complex
challenges and intense crises that confronted his regime. As is
often noted, Nicholas was a devoted husband and ideal father,
and he could exert considerable personal charm. But his qualifications for leadership of a huge and seething society were almost nil.
Not broadly educated, little interested in people and politics,
encased in the attitudes and prejudices of his royal and noble
milieu, he found it difficult even to comprehend, let alone adjust
to, the changes taking place in Russian society. In November
1914, with Russia already deeply involved in World War I,
Nicholas toured the Caucasus, an area soon to be torn by social
and ethnic strife, and wrote to his wife:

> [The people] are beginning to be wealthy, and above all they
> have an inconceivably high number of small infants. All future
> subjects. This all fills me with joy and faith in God's mercy.
> I look forward in peace and confidence to what lies in store for
> Russia.[2]

Although Nicholas worked reasonably hard at affairs of state,
he was by turns indecisive and capricious. He could be madden-
ingly stubborn and at times displayed a dogged and unshakable
faith in the virtue of his autocratic position. Often his personal
whims affected his decisions; for example, he frequently retained
or appointed ministers and personal advisers at court not on the
basis of their qualifications but because he liked them. Nicholas's
snobbish dislike of Witte, the ablest Russian statesman of the

---

[2] *The Letters of the Tsar to the Tsaritsa, 1914–17,* trans. A. L. Hynes
(London and New York, 1929), p. 16.

period, played a part in the tsar's dismissal of Witte as prime minister in April 1906.

As peasants and workers became both more desperate and more sophisticated on the eve of revolution, many of them came to blame the tsar for failing to ameliorate their lot. But they were also alienated by what the tsar did do, particularly such events as Bloody Sunday at the start of the Revolution of 1905, when troops fired on a large crowd of unarmed petitioners marching to the palace to present their grievances to the tsar. That Nicholas was away and largely unaware of what was transpiring did not matter; as a personal autocrat he was held responsible by the educated and uneducated alike. Nicholas's personal support of military expeditions sent to the countryside in 1905 and 1906 to suppress rebellious peasants by force and his government's brutal quelling of such labor disturbances as the strike in the Lena gold mines in 1912 also turned the people against the tsar.

The events of the war were decisive in this regard. The Russian government's decision in early August 1914 to go to war with Germany and Austria-Hungary was greeted with patriotic fervor and general enthusiasm by almost everyone in Russia. Few foresaw the length and brutality of the struggle, and no one expected defeat. Whether winning would have made any difference is a moot point. To be sure, it would have been harder to replace a victorious government; but even as a winner Russian society could hardly have emerged from World War I without being profoundly altered. The main revolutionary impact of the war was the enormous strain it imposed on the system as a whole and the overwhelming burdens it forced the people to bear. After a time this combination made Tsar Nicholas's position untenable.

As before the war, people came increasingly to blame the tsar for the terrible things that happened and for the fact that good things didn't. Many held Nicholas responsible for the grief, suffering, and fear the war brought: "If the tsar were a good tsar, why couldn't he save Russia and its people?" And Nicholas's actions did not help matters. He associated himself personally with the war effort, finally making himself commander-in-chief of the

Russian army and moving to general headquarters at the front to oversee operations. The tsar came to symbolize the failures and hardships of the war.

In addition, the civilian government responsible to Nicholas became an object of contempt and hatred among both the politically articulate and the masses. Neither the institutions nor the social and economic systems of Russia could have withstood the strains of a long, wasting, and immense military struggle over hundreds of miles, involving millions of men and billions of dollars. But the situation was made much worse by the incompetence and moral corruption of the government. It was bad enough to suffer and to lose, but to do so in part because the country was being run by a clique of second-raters and sycophants was intolerable. In fact, the government so badly mismanaged the war effort that a leading liberal in the Duma, Professor Paul N. Miliukov, delivered a major attack on the government entitled "Is This Folly, or Treason?" It certainly was not treason, but the record of the administration was so poor as to elicit such suspicions, not only among politicians but among all classes of the population.

The last straw, which erased any vestiges of popular loyalty to the tsar, was the nefarious influence of Grigory Efimovich Rasputin—a self-proclaimed "holy man"—in court circles and on the government itself. Nicholas's wife, the Tsarina Alexandra, displayed intense maternal concern over the only son born to the royal couple, the Tsarevitch Alexis, who had hemophilia, a hereditary and incurable bleeding disease. Alexandra, a woman of mystical bent, sought help for her son not only in the medical profession but among quacks and religious healers. On several occasions before the war, Alexis's condition had temporarily improved after Rasputin's prayers and ministrations; in this way Rasputin acquired great influence with Alexandra. But because of his uncouth and disreputable behavior in St. Petersburg society, Rasputin was for a time sent out of the capital.

During the stress of wartime he returned, and when Tsar Nicholas went to the front, Tsarina Alexandra and, through her, Rasputin acquired considerable authority in governmental affairs.

Tsar Nicholas II, a devoted father but weak ruler, with his family.
Keystone Press Agency Inc.

Despite his unsavory reputation, Rasputin was able to influence appointments to positions in the administration and the tsarina was prepared to listen to him even on policy matters, as the following excerpt from one of her letters to Nicholas shows: "I fully trust in our Friend's [Rasputin's] wisdom endowed by God, to counsel what is right for you and our country. He sees far ahead and therefore his judgement can be relied upon."[3]

Rasputin's role finally became such a scandal that in December 1916 a group of nobles and conservatives murdered him, though not without difficulty, in an effort to salvage the good name of the government and the royal family. The murder plot called for Rasputin to be invited for supper at the home of Prince Yusopov, a member of a leading family in Russian society and one of the conspirators. Although the plotters poisoned, shot, and beat Rasputin, he managed somehow to stay alive and staggered after his attackers, frothing at the mouth. Finally they threw him into a nearby river, where he drowned. But although Rasputin was gone, the damage to the regime had been done, and few people in Petrograd or the country at large now felt anything but disgust or contempt for the tsarist autocracy. As a cousin of Nicholas's put it, "The government itself is busily paving the way for revolution."

WAS THE REVOLUTION INEVITABLE?

This review of some of the basic causes of the revolution has not resolved the intriguing, though unanswerable, question: Was the Russian Revolution inevitable? Could Russian society have changed gradually without the sudden radical shift of direction that 1917 brought? Soviet and some Western writers have maintained that the popular grievances, class divisions, and institutional weaknesses of Russian society were too extensive and deep-seated for reform and peaceful evolution to take place.[4] Other observers

---

[3] *Letters of the Tsaritsa to the Tsar* (New York, 1924), p. 390.

[4] See, for example, Leopold Haimson, "The Problem of Social Stability in Urban Russia, 1905–1917," *Slavic Review,* 23, no. 4 (1964), 620–642; and 24, no. 1 (1965), 1–22.

have treated the issue of inevitability as a series of "iffy" postulates: if Russia had not become involved in World War I, there would have been no revolution; if Tsar Nicholas II had been stronger and more farsighted, there would have been no revolution; if the top leaders of the tsarist government had been more receptive to change and the system itself had not been so rigid, there would have been no revolution; and so on. In such analyses it is usually difficult to tell which variable is the crucial one, the absence of which made the revolution inevitable.

Other explanations of the revolution focus on even broader issues. Some believe that the tsarist system and leadership were not only ineffective but so incapable of providing decent humane governance as to be immoral and beyond redemption. Others point to the basic despair of the masses and their hatred of the old rulers and system as the crucial factors bringing on the revolution. Still others see Russian society as lacking the resilience, the level of development, and the critical stratum of enlightened leaders necessary for it to undergo the shocks of modernization without violence and revolution.

As with so many historical issues, although no answer can be given to the question of whether Russia was fated to experience a revolution, the very process of puzzling over a solution helps to clarify the basic factors facilitating and blocking change in Russian society. In this way the long-term and proximate causes of the revolution become more sharply defined. At the same time, the question remains: Without World War I, would Russia have exploded in revolution, or would that vast country have gradually evolved into an industrialized, stable society with some measure of popular participation in its management?

2
The February Revolution: Collapse of the Old Order

★

THE PEOPLE DECIDE

The day was cloudy and gray, but it was warmer than it had been much of the winter, when at times the thermometer had stuck at 25 or 30 degrees below zero and a bone-chilling wind had swept off the Gulf of Finland to swirl along the streets of Petrograd. Spring was still some weeks away, and people were dispirited and miserable. The last few months had been a continuous battle to make ends meet in the face of rising prices and to find enough fuel and food to keep from freezing and starving. The losing, senseless war was a constant depressing weight on everyone's shoulders. And no one had confidence in either the government or the tsar.

It was March 8, 1917, International Women's Day, a socialist holiday celebrated by various groups and individuals on the streets of Russia's capital. Also on the streets were several thousand workers who had been locked out of the Putilov factory because of a labor dispute. Moreover, the long lines that had formed in front of bread stores the past few days were even longer and more restless today. The atmosphere was tense and expectant. A few meetings were held and speeches made. Red banners proclaiming

"DOWN WITH THE AUTOCRACY" appeared here and there. Occasionally the demonstrators clashed with the police. But people were clearly waiting, indeed hoping, for something to happen that would break the drab and wretched routine of their wintry existence. It was hard to see what could happen, yet the milling crowds appeared increasingly confident that something would.

The next day, March 9, strikes spread throughout the city. Textile workers, printers, and machinists quit work and joined others already in the streets. The tens of thousands of the previous day swelled to almost 200,000. The air of expectation intensified, and the demonstrators became increasingly bold and restive. No agitators, no leaders, could be observed. Avoiding police guards at the bridges over the Neva River, crowds crossed on the ice to mill aimlessly in the center of the city. They were hostile to the police but friendly with soldiers.

On March 10 the crowds continued to grow as a general strike was called and students left schools and universities to join the demonstrators. The ordinary life of Petrograd became increasingly paralyzed. Bread stores closed, trolleys stopped running, papers were not published, schools were recessed. The old system was simply ceasing to function. Nevertheless, Tsarina Alexandra (calling to mind Marie Antoinette's alleged remark about crowds who were demanding bread during the French Revolution, "Let them eat cake") wrote to her husband concerning the people thronging the streets of Petrograd: "If the weather were very cold, they would all probably stay at home."[1]

On March 11 the government began to respond. The tsar sent instructions from his headquarters at the front for the disorders in the streets to be suppressed. Police and troops opened fire on demonstrators in several places, killing more than one hundred. Some one hundred radicals, including five Bolshevik leaders, were arrested. The prime minister used a signed but undated tsarist decree to dissolve the Duma. The president of the Duma, M. V. Rodzianko, dispatched telegrams to Nicholas protesting this action

---

[1] Quoted in William Henry Chamberlin, *The Russian Revolution, 1917–1921* (2 vols., New York, 1935; reprinted 1965), I, p. 73.

and urging formation of a new government of public confidence in order to save the dynasty and the country, but the tsar merely commented to an aide, "This fat Rodzianko has sent me some nonsense to which I will not even reply."[2] By evening, further plans to put down the disturbances began to be implemented.

As conditions in Petrograd and other cities had worsened during the winter, military authorities responsible for security behind the lines had worked out procedures for suppressing urban unrest should it get out of hand. The first line of defense was to be the police and the Cossacks (a special force of mounted troops used by the last few tsars to break up strikes and quell revolutionary disturbances). Army units were to be used as a last resort, because although there were 180,000 troops in the Petrograd garrison, only some 12,000 were considered reliable. During the days of March 10 and 11 the demonstrators seemed deliberately to be joshing and playing up to the Cossacks and soldiers, who often responded sympathetically. Two regiments had fired on the crowds on March 11, and it was decided to employ additional army units to disperse the demonstrators on March 12. However, early in the morning of March 12, soldiers of one of the regiments employed the day before, after talking all night about what they had done, decided they would not shoot at the crowds again and soon mutinied against their officers. Moreover, soldiers in several other regiments refused to carry out the authorities' orders to suppress the crowds by force. By the afternoon of March 12 a good part of the garrison had mutinied, and the soldiers, as well as a few officers, began to fraternize with or actually to join the crowds.

This was the decisive moment of the February Revolution. The tsarist government had no other support on which to call once the army had failed it. During the Revolution of 1905, when disorders had been far more widespread, including an armed uprising in Moscow, the government had survived because it had been able to draw upon loyal troops. In March 1917 the government's only possible recourse after the garrison troops in Petrograd had

[2] *Ibid.*, p. 78.

mutinied or dissolved into the crowds was to order in seasoned units from the front. Indeed, a small force was directed against Petrograd, but its troops also went over to the revolutionaries. Moreover, most of the senior officers, led by General Alekseev, chief of staff of the army, were fed up with the ineffectual tsar and his bumbling ministers and preferred a government that would have popular support and would be more effective in organizing the war effort.

By the evening of March 12 it was all over. The tsarist ministers were soon arrested by a revolutionary committee, and the central authority of the old government simply disappeared almost without a trace. It was a complete and cherished victory for the people. The cost was not high; there were about 1,400 casualties in Petrograd and few in the rest of the country. As William Henry Chamberlin put it in his classic history of the revolution: "The collapse of the Romanov autocracy in March 1917 was one of the most leaderless, spontaneous, anonymous revolutions of all time."[3]

The February Revolution was neither unexpected nor inevitable, but it was indeed sudden and elemental. As we saw earlier, at the time of Russia's decision to go to war, some individuals had predicted that the system could not stand the strain of a long war. From the late summer of 1916, when it became clear that the incompetence of the ministers and the blindness of the tsar were irreversible defects, observers of all political persuasions had declared that the government could not last. The following fall and winter saw considerable talk and some dreamy scheming among both conservative and liberal politicians—and even by a few highly placed generals—concerning the necessity to terminate the political meddling of the tsarina, to shunt aside or replace the tsar, and to form a new government that could act decisively and efficiently, thereby regaining the confidence of the people. But no viable plots were hatched, and no one took the concrete steps necessary to bring about change, although a few conservatives succeeded

[3] *Ibid.,* p. 73.

in murdering Rasputin. As a result, the events of March 8 through 12 in Petrograd, planned and directed by no one, surprised everyone. And frightened some, too; the comments of Andrei I. Shingarev, a liberal Duma member, typified the qualms felt by some thoughtful Russians as they tried to digest the meaning of the February Revolution:

> Until the last I continued to hope that they [the government] would somehow see the light and make concessions. But no, they dismissed the Duma. . . . Any agreement with the Duma, no matter what kind, was the last chance to escape revolution. . . . If the Duma is brushed aside, then we are face to face with the street.[4]

The rapid and total collapse of the old regime can only be explained by those factors discussed in Chapter One: the uprooting, disillusionment, and suffering caused by the war; the injustices of the regime; the breakdown of the economy; and the thorough discrediting of the tsardom during the course of Nicholas's reign. When the people came out aimlessly into the streets of Petrograd, testifying that they could bear no more, there was no one to divert or stop them. Hardly a single individual acted, or even spoke out, in defense of the government. It vanished because the overwhelming majority of the Russian people simply couldn't live under it any longer. There has seldom been such a clear, effective, and yet unconscious expression of collective will in recent times. No one told the people of Petrograd what to do. They were themselves moved to act—and changed the course of history.

POLITICAL PATCHWORK

Once the significance of the events in Petrograd had become clear, no one believed Nicholas could be retained as tsar. A few

---

[4] Cited from the memoirs of V. V. Shulgin in Roger Pethybridge (ed.), *Witnesses to the Russian Revolution* (London, 1964), p. 104.

people, however, thought it worthwhile to try to preserve the monarchy, some because they felt that legal and psychological continuity in the government was important to the war effort and might help avert disorder and chaos, and some because they believed a constitutional monarchy would be best for the country. As a result, on March 15 two Duma leaders went to army head-quarters to talk to the bewildered Nicholas. Since the army com-manders had already counseled abdication, Nicholas was quite ready to give up the throne. At first he intended to abdicate in favor of his son, Alexis, but after the court physician reminded him that the tsarevitch would never recover from his hemophilia, the tsar decided to transfer the crown instead to his brother, the Grand Duke Michael. This arrangement, which the populace would probably have rejected in any case, soon broke down. Michael refused to become tsar after he learned that the Duma leaders could not guarantee his safety or the continuance of the tsardom.

It is a measure of Nicholas's limited capabilities and his lack of touch with reality that the day after he abdicated the 300-year-old throne of the Romanovs and accepted the complete collapse of his rule over a vast country, he could write in his diary on his way to a safe place of detention: "I had a long sound sleep. Woke up beyond Dvinsk. Sunshine and frost . . . I read much of Julius Caesar."

Nicholas and his family met a tragic fate. Though some pro-posed sending him into exile in England, socialist leaders opposed this, fearing that he might become there a rallying point for monarchists and counterrevolutionaries. After spending some fairly pleasant months of quiet family life under mild "house arrest" in Siberia, Nicholas, Alexandra, their four daughters, and Alexis found themselves in July 1918 in the path of advancing counter-revolutionary forces determined to overthrow the Soviet govern-ment that had come to power in the fall of 1917. The members of the royal family were moved once, and then, on local initiative, were brutally murdered to prevent their being captured by anti-Soviet detachments. Despite the legend that one of the daughters, Grand Duchess Anastasia, escaped, the evidence is overwhelming that the entire family perished. The Bolshevik leaders of the Soviet government in Moscow, though they did not order this execution, were indifferent when informed of what had happened.

In March 1917, even before it became clear that any form of the tsarist system, however modified, was unacceptable to the people, steps had been taken to work out an alternative. On March 12, the day after the dismissal of the Duma, most of its members convened anyway in the Tauride Palace, their usual meeting place. Technically they did not defy the tsar's order of March 11 dismissing the Duma since they met in a private room. They established a temporary committee to exercise authority in the absence of any government, and that committee soon appointed a provisional government, a cabinet of ministers drawn largely from the moderate parties in the Duma.

The Provisional government, which lasted for eight months, operated at all times under three major disabilities. First, its own members and most of the educated public considered it a temporary and transitional government. There was some uncertainty about its being the legal heir of the tsarist government, but in any case it was made clear from the outset that the Provisional government was to rule only until all the people of Russia could express their will. Plans were made for a democratically elected Constituent Assembly which would decide the future form of government for the nation. As a result, the Provisional government was truly *provisional*, which hampered its ability to act decisively on issues affecting the future structure and policies of Russian society. The masses, while some favored the democratic principle that lay behind the government's hesitancy, could never understand why the Provisional government did not act more vigorously to solve the people's immediate problems.

The second disability, resulting in part from the first, was that the Provisional government was never able to establish firm authority in the country. A number of factors worked against it in this regard. Even before the February Revolution, the centralized tsarist administration had begun to disintegrate under the impact of the war and as a result of growing nationalism in non-Russian areas. The Provisional government was not strong enough to reform and resurrect this far-flung bureaucratic system. Besides, from the very beginning it had to compete for power with the soviets, or Councils of Workers' and Soldiers' Deputies, which were set up immediately in Petrograd and not long thereafter in most areas of Russia. Further, it had little control over the peasantry. Once the latter decided that they did not like the new structure of local administration and the land policies of the Provisional government, they ignored the central authorities and did as they pleased.

Finally, the Provisional government was in part a victim of the general intoxication with freedom that followed the February Revolution. As we shall see in the next chapter, Russians of all stripes took the revolution as a signal to rebel against all forms of authority.

A serious structural weakness of the Provisional government was that it was always an amalgam of divergent groups and leaders. This was the case even when it was first formed. The premier was Prince G. Lvov, a respected nonparty figure who had headed the All-Russian Union of Zemstvos (local units of self-government). Professor Paul N. Miliukov, leader of the major liberal party, the Kadets (Constitutional Democrats), was minister for foreign affairs, and several members of the more conservative Octobrist Party also held posts. The cabinet was rounded out with one mild leftist, Alexander F. Kerensky, who was later to become prime minister, and a few nonparty people. It was a mixed leadership at best. Later cabinets included moderate socialists as well.

The evening the Provisional government was formed, an exciting, noisy, and momentous meeting was held in another part of the Tauride Palace. Attending were representatives of various workers' groups, a few socialist and radical politicians, and some soldiers who had been prominent in the events of the past few days. There was a good deal of wild talk, lots of smoke and enthusiasm, some stem-winding speeches, and finally a decision to reestablish the Petrograd Soviet, first formed during the Revolution of 1905. At that time workers in several towns near Moscow had set up ad hoc committees to direct strikes, apparently on the model of the assembly of heads of households that operated traditionally in many Russian peasant villages. These committees were successful in representing the workers' interests and soon evolved into Soviets (Councils) of Workers' Deputies in major cities, including Petrograd (then St. Petersburg) and Moscow. The soviets had been a key institution in the Revolution of 1905, and though they were suppressed after the revolution, their utility was remembered in March 1917 as the old order collapsed.

Because of the important part soldiers played in the revolution, when the Petrograd Soviet was reborn on March 12, it soon became the Soviet of Workers' *and* Soldiers' Deputies. Delegates were selected roughly on the basis of one for each thousand workers and one from each company of soldiers. The body itself chose an executive committee of fifteen members, dominated by the Mensheviks and Socialist Revolutionaries.

Both the Mensheviks and the Bolsheviks were radical Marxists, members of the Russian Social Democratic Labor Party (RSDLP). At the Second Congress of the RSDLP in 1903 two groups within the party had disagreed over several matters of policy. The most significant was the nature of the party: Lenin and his followers wanted it to be a small, elite, highly disciplined band of professional revolutionaries; his opponents favored a larger, broadly based, more open party. Lenin's faction was actually a minority at the Congress, but on one key vote they won a majority and quickly took for themselves the psychologically useful designation *Bolsheviks* ("majority-ites"). Their opponents, always a majority in the social democratic movement until the fall of 1917, were stuck with the name *Mensheviks* ("minority-ites"). In 1912 the Bolsheviks declared themselves an independent party, the RSDLP(B), and despite efforts at reunification during the war and in 1917, Lenin kept the Bolsheviks separate. The different attitudes and policies of these two Marxist parties in 1917 will be discussed in the next chapter.

A few days after its formation the executive committee of the Petrograd Soviet decided that it would not actively oppose the

Provisional government but would tolerate its existence as a way of preserving and advancing the revolution. As we shall see shortly, however, the Soviet and the Provisional government differed on a number of issues. Moreover, from the beginning the Soviet exercised considerable authority, quite independently of the Provisional government, in such areas as management of communications, city housing, provisioning, and grievances within the army.

PETROGRAD, MARCH 1917

What was it like to live through the tumultuous days of the February Revolution? The following eyewitness accounts convey some of the exhilaration, uncertainty, and bewilderment many citizens felt:

> The trolleys are not running. There are no more horsecabs. We went with mother to see the girls [at school]. The streets were calm but full of people. After our visit . . . we decided to cross the Nevsky [main street of Petrograd], but after we had gone a hundred paces, gunfire broke out . . . The gunfire became more and more violent. In order to avoid being crushed by the mob we hurried to Semenovsky Street. [Letter of Dmitri Shakhovskoi, fourteen-year-old scion of a noble family.][5]

> I looked out; there was no one on the bridge which usually presents a busy scene. But almost immediately, a disorderly mob carrying red flags appeared at the end . . . on the right bank of the Neva [River] and a regiment came towards them from the opposite side. It looked as if there would be a violent collision, but on the contrary, the two bodies coalesced. The army was fraternizing with the revolution.[6]

> In the Catherine Hall and the antechamber [of the Tauride Palace, meeting place of the Duma] soldiers, arms in hand, were

[5] Dmitri von Mohrenschildt (ed.), *The Russian Revolution of 1917: Contemporary Accounts* (New York, 1971), p. 103.

[6] Maurice Paleologue, *An Ambassador's Memoirs* (New York, 1925), III, p. 221.

standing in groups or columns where someone had drawn them up in orderly, but loose, formation. Others had stacked their arms and were sitting on the floor supping on bread, herrings, and tea. Others, finally, were already asleep, stretched out on the floor like third-class passengers huddled together for warmth in railway stations. . . .

Sacks of meal had been heaped into a pile a step or two from the entrance. Near them stood two obedient guards, just like those posted by Tsarist officers, who didn't show the slightest sign of understanding what was taking place around them. "Whom are they obeying and why?" flashed through my mind. . . .

One's feet slid on the floor, where mud and snow were mingled. Chaos was everywhere. There was a merciless draught through the door from the street, and a reek of soldiers' boots and greatcoats. [From the memoirs of N. N. Sukhanov, a Socialist Revolutionary.][7]

THE FEBRUARY REVOLUTION OUTSIDE PETROGRAD

When news of the collapse of the old government and creation of the Provisional government reached Moscow, workers' groups there called a strike in support of the revolution and began disarming policemen. This succeeded in almost completely halting the usual activities of the city. Shortly thereafter, the governor general and other tsarist authorities willingly relinquished control of Moscow to the hastily formed Committee of Public Organizations. There was no fighting, no resistance, and the citizens of Moscow welcomed the revolution enthusiastically.

In most of the provincial centers, towns, and villages throughout the empire, news of the events in Petrograd was sufficient to trigger "a revolution." Power passed effortlessly from local authorities to improvised committees of leading citizens, lawyers, journalists, and local representatives of moderate political parties, or in some cases to soviets created on the model of the Petrograd Soviet. In this regard Leon Trotsky, a prominent Bolshevik leader

[7] Pethybridge, *Witnesses to the Russian Revolution,* pp. 112–113.

later in 1917 and author of an absorbing but naturally partisan *History of the Russian Revolution*, recounts a delightful, if perhaps apocryphal, tale: "In Kharkov, the chief of police, having gone to the railroad station and got news of the revolution, stood up in his carriage before an excited crowd and, lifting his hat, shouted at the top of his lungs: 'Long live the Revolution! Hurrah!' "[8] In Tver crowds marched through the streets singing the song of the French Revolution, "La Marseillaise," although this procession later degenerated into rioting and the provincial governor was killed. In several regions of the empire where non-Russians predominated, the revolutionary transfer of power was to committees or groups which favored greater autonomy for their area.

FOREIGN REACTION TO THE FEBRUARY REVOLUTION

Outside of Russia the revolutionary upheaval was greeted warmly on all sides. Russia's enemies, Germany and Austria-Hungary, believed, as eventually proved to be the case, that the revolution would weaken the Russian war effort and make its military defeat easier. Russia's allies, France and England, were on the whole pleased because their leaders had always found it uncomfortable to be defending democracy against German militarism shoulder to shoulder with the autocratic and backward empire of the tsars. Public opinion in the West was delighted no longer to have the monarchical embarrassment of tsarism and looked forward to a strengthened and reinvigorated Russia carrying the war forward to a glorious victory.

Allied diplomats and politicians, though optimistic, had a somewhat more balanced view than the masses of the meaning of the February Revolution. They were glad, of course, to be rid not only of the political liability of Nicholas's regime but also of his inept and bumbling government, and they hoped the Russians could now reverse the tide of defeat on the Eastern Front. At the same time, they were well aware that the revolution, unless controlled, could

[8] Leon Trotsky, *History of the Russian Revolution* (London, 1965), I, p. 142.

easily lead to an unraveling of Russian society and perhaps even to Russia's withdrawal from the war. As the views of the British Foreign Office were reported to Petrograd: "The Government is animated by a sincere desire to render . . . all possible aid and assistance to the Provisional Government. . . . On the other hand, there is very definite concern over the stability of the present provisional regime."[9]

In the United States the downfall of the tsar was greeted with jubilation. Within a few weeks the United States would enter the war on the Allied side, and President Woodrow Wilson, his advisers, and the American press were much relieved that they would be fighting alongside democratic, not reactionary, Russia. Wilson himself declared in early April:

> Russia was known by those who knew it best to have been always in fact democratic at heart. . . . The autocracy . . . was not in fact Russian in origin, character, or purpose; and now it has been shaken off and the great, generous Russian people have been added in all their native majesty and might to the forces that are fighting for freedom in the world, for justice, and for peace.[10]

FIRST STEPS OF THE NEW GOVERNMENT

For the Provisional government, the most pressing question was Russia's role in World War I. With hindsight we can see that the war was an immediate cause of the revolution and that the population was obviously sick of it by the spring of 1917. But at the time inertia, the lingering effects of patriotism, a concern for national survival, and a sense of duty to Russia's allies all combined to make it unthinkable, both for the leaders of the new government and for many among the revolutionary crowds, that Russia should withdraw from the war. Some were concerned about what

[9] Robert Paul Browder and Alexander F. Kerensky (eds.), *The Russian Provisional Government 1917: Documents* (Stanford, Calif., 1961), II, p. 1050.

[10] Ray Stannard Baker and William E. Dodd (eds.), *The Public Papers of Woodrow Wilson* (New York and London, 1927), V, pp. 12–13.

sort of victory Russia should seek and how she should achieve it, but among the slogans of the time, like "Down with autocracy," "Bread," and "Long live the revolution," none yet demanded immediate peace.

The moderate and liberal groups represented in the Provisional government wanted Russia not only to continue the war but to improve its record therein, if possible reversing the recent series of losses and pushing the Austrians and Germans out of Russian territory. Some supporters of the government believed that it was appropriate to redefine and restate Russia's war aims, but there was no agreement on what these should now be. A few felt that Russia should not seek any foreign territory as a prize of the war, while others were convinced that the Provisional government should seize the chance to make clear exactly what concessions and rewards it expected, such as control of the Turkish Straits and Constantinople, which had been promised to Russia in secret treaties concluded among the Allies in 1915.

On taking office the Provisional government simply reaffirmed its support of the Allied cause and its adherence to the military and diplomatic commitments of the overthrown tsarist government. The issue of the war was not as clearly resolved in the Petrograd Soviet. World War I had been a terrible blow to the international socialist movement, which had always opposed war and urged workers to direct their energies to the struggle against capitalism. But in 1914 most socialists in Europe had followed a patriotic line and supported their own national governments in the war effort. Lenin and a few other leftists had vigorously opposed the war under the slogan, "Turn the imperialist war into a civil war," but they were considered a radical fringe of socialism. With the Bolsheviks a small minority in the Petrograd Soviet, policy toward the war was largely determined by the Menshevik majority. Although there were several schools of thought on this issue among the Mensheviks, the dominant position was that Russia must continue the struggle against German militarism but with a different set of war aims. In particular the Mensheviks urged that the Allies renounce annexations of foreign territory and indemnities (payments by the defeated to the victors) as objectives of the struggle. This was the position the Petrograd Soviet eventually adopted in a statement of March 27 to the "Peoples of the whole world," which declared: "The time has come to begin a decisive struggle with the acquisitive aspirations of the governments of other countries. . . . In the consciousness of its revolutionary strength the Russian democracy . . . summons the peoples of Europe to decisive manifestations in favor of peace."[11]

A small group of Mensheviks was not satisfied that this went far enough and pressed for the beginning of peace negotiations. The Bolsheviks then in Petrograd accepted the Soviet's position for the time being, while urging in their newspaper, *Pravda*, on March 30, "pressure on the Provisional Government with the demand that it consent to the immediate opening of peace talks."[12] As we shall see in the next chapter, it was only after Lenin's return to Russia from exile in Switzerland that the Bolshevik party began to demand peace.

A second major issue for the Provisional government was how to respond to the growing demands of non-Russian nationalities within the empire. The government recognized the right of the Poles to become an independent nation after the war; this was easy to do because the Germans and Austrians occupied all of what had been Russian Poland before the war. At the same time, Finland was granted full autonomy. But the Provisional government was unable to adopt a clear-cut position in respect to other groups. The parties represented in the government generally believed in a centralized Russian state, with perhaps some autonomy for non-Russian groups; but none of them intended to preside over the dissolution of the Russian empire. Thus the Provisional government abolished old legal restrictions based on religion or nationality, which particularly benefited the Jews, a special target of tsarist discrimination, but left unsettled its future policy on the political rights of minorities within the Russian polity.

Some key political questions were quickly resolved. The new government proclaimed the inviolability of basic civil liberties,

---

[11] Quoted in Chamberlin, I, 108.

[12] Quoted in Robert C. Tucker, *Stalin as Revolutionary, 1879–1929* (New York, 1973), p. 164.

the end of political censorship, and an amnesty for political and religious prisoners. It guaranteed freedom to join unions and to strike, as well as the right of all Russian citizens to participate in the planned elections for a Constituent Assembly. It proposed replacement of the police by a people's militia and new free elections for all units of local administration. In all these measures it had the support of the Petrograd Soviet.

When it came to social issues, however, the Provisional government was unable to agree on a detailed program with the executive committee of the Petrograd Soviet. The latter demanded an eight-hour workday, higher wages, provisions to ban lockouts, and improved insurance and welfare benefits. At this juncture neither group was prepared to outline a definitive policy toward agriculture and the needs of the peasants.

A central issue for both the Provisional government and the Petrograd Soviet was their mutual relations. Each body exercised some authority, in an awkward arrangement that came to be known as "dual power." The Provisional government was well aware that it was dependent to some extent on the Soviet since so many soldiers and skilled workers in key fields would act only on the orders of the Soviet. The situation was well summed up, if in a slightly exaggerated way, in a letter from the minister of war to the army commander on March 22:

> The Provisional Government possesses no real power and its orders are executed only in so far as this is permitted by the Soviet of Workers' and Soldiers' Deputies, which holds in its hands the most important elements of actual power, such as troops, railroads, postal and telegraph service. It is possible to say directly that the Provisional Government exists only while this is permitted by the soviet.[13]

The leaders of the Provisional government were not happy with this situation but accepted it as a temporary and necessary by-product of the revolution.

The Soviet leaders, mostly moderate socialists, were ideologi-

[13] Quoted in Chamberlin, I, 101.

cally disposed to cooperate with the Provisional government. Marxist theory taught that before a proletarian socialist revolution could occur in Russia there had to be a capitalist, or "bourgeois-democratic," revolution. Russia needed to pass through a capitalist stage of history before moving on to the final historical stage of socialism. Since for the Russian socialists the February Revolution was the long-expected "bourgeois-democratic" revolution, doctrine encouraged them to support that revolution, using the freedom it would bring to proselytize the workers in preparation for a later socialist revolution. Lenin had a somewhat different view, as we shall see in the next chapter; but the Bolsheviks in Petrograd when the February Revolution occurred, after briefly taking a more radical line, went along with the dominant socialist view of the Provisional government.

After brief, wary, but generally conciliatory negotiations, the Petrograd Soviet agreed to support the Provisional government as long as it "fulfills its promises and effectively combats the old regime." Although the Soviet leaders opposed socialist participation in the Provisional government, they officially overlooked the fact that Alexander F. Kerensky, a former Duma deputy and a member of the Soviet executive committee, chose to join the new cabinet as a private citizen.

By the end of March a viable, if precarious, new order had been established. The interests of the liberals and moderates were directly represented in the Provisional government and those of the urban masses indirectly through the Petrograd Soviet's acquiescence in the new regime. There was no trace of the old order in the leadership of the central institutions. The unplanned outburst of the Petrograd masses a few weeks previously seemed to have had the almost miraculous results of firmly and forever rejecting the image of tsarism and establishing an era of liberation and progress for the Russian people. But what did the new freedom mean, and how were Russians to use it? Answers to these questions began to take shape in the next few months.

Table 2. RELATIONS BETWEEN THE PROVISIONAL GOVERNMENT AND THE PETROGRAD SOVIET

PROVISIONAL GOVERNMENT	PETROGRAD SOVIET

Points of Agreement

Both favor:

continuing the war
abolition of racial or religious
  discrimination
end of censorship
civil liberties
freeing of political prisoners
right to form unions and to trade
elections to a constituent assembly
reorganization of local government
final land reform must await
  constituent assembly

Points of Disagreement

PG favors:

original war aims, including
  territorial acquisitions
gradual shortening of workday
labor discipline to bolster war
  production
tax policies to stimulate production

Areas of Control or Influence

ministries; executive organizations
judiciary
army high command
foreign trade
war production

Points of Disagreement

Soviet favors:

war aim of peace without
  annexations or indemnities
eight-hour workday
higher wages and benefits
social reforms
end of lockouts

Areas of Control or Influence

railways
post and telegraph
garrison troops
factory committees
unions
local housing

3
The Meaning of Liberation
★

RETURN OF THE EXILES: VLADIMIR ILICH LENIN

As the train jerked slowly to a stop, a sizable crowd pressed forward on the platform. There were dignitaries in long coats and fur hats (for it was still cold in Petrograd on April 16); alongside them stood workers in blouses and felt boots and soldiers and sailors in uniform. A young girl was pushed forward ready to deliver a bouquet of flowers. Hardly had the steam from the locomotive evaporated and the grinding of its brakes ceased when a small group of men and women descended from the train, and a band began to play.

The travelers were escorted into a waiting room, and the welcoming speeches began. The chairman of the executive committee of the Petrograd Soviet concluded his remarks with, "We consider that the chief task of revolutionary democracy [i.e., the Soviet] at present is to defend our Revolution against all attacks from within no less than from without. This requires not disunity but the closing of democratic ranks." A short stocky man with a beard and intense piercing eyes replied briefly; then, moving outside, he declared to a waiting crowd: "The world-wide socialist revolution has already dawned. . . . the Russian Revolution . . . has paved the way and opened a new epoch. Long live the world-wide socialist revolution." Bewildered by these extremist words, the crowd nevertheless gave the speaker a genuinely warm welcome. Vladimir Ilich Lenin, the leader of the Bolsheviks, had returned to Russia from exile.

Similar scenes were enacted many times in the first few months of the revolution. Lenin's homecoming was, of course, a special case, but for many Russian revolutionaries the most important immediate consequence of the February Revolution was their release from prison or the opportunity to return from exile, whether in Siberia or abroad. Political activists of all kinds flooded back to the major cities, especially Moscow and Petrograd. Joseph V. Stalin and Lev B. Kamenev, prominent Bolsheviks, came by train from central Siberia, Leon Trotsky by boat from the United States —after a short delay caused by British hesitancy in granting him a transit visa—and Lenin and other prominent radicals by train through Germany and Scandinavia from Switzerland.

Lenin's trip home was later to acquire some notoriety, including charges that he was a German agent. As soon as news of the February Revolution reached Switzerland, where Lenin had been living since 1913, he fretted to get back to Russia. The quickest way was across Germany, although some of the Russian radicals in exile in Switzerland were reluctant to take this route because they detested the militaristic government of Germany. Lenin, however, considered the Allied and German leaders equally bad since to him all of them were imperialist oppressors of the proletariat; he was happy to accept assistance from any quarter as long as such aid hastened his entry on the Russian revolutionary scene. Lenin hoped that if the revolution in Russia could be deepened and extended into a proletarian revolution, it might spark socialist revolutions in Europe that would overthrow both the German and Allied governments. Thus, to Lenin, the German regime, in helping him, was abetting the international socialist revolution and digging its own grave.

For their part, the German authorities were not then worried about revolution spreading from Russia to Germany. Instead, they were anxious to do anything that might cause new unrest inside Russia, thereby further weakening their enemy to the east and permitting Germany to concentrate more forces against the Allies on the Western Front. The German leaders saw Lenin and other revolutionaries abroad as probable troublemakers—as indeed they were. And the German government wanted to be sure that on their way back to Russia Lenin and his radical colleagues did not infect the German people with revolutionary germs. Thus they agreed to send Lenin and others from Switzerland across Germany in what came to be called the "sealed" train. It was, of course, not actually sealed; rather, its revolutionary passengers were enjoined from making speeches, passing out literature, or having any contact with the public as the train traversed German territory. The group of Russian radicals readily agreed to this condition, passed across Germany uneventfully, and made their way home through Sweden and Finland.

Lenin's return to Russia was a turning point in the history of the revolution. This was not so much because of what he did at once or because of the first impression he made; rather, it was because of his personal qualities as a leader and because of what he fervently believed. Lenin, born Vladimir Ilich Ulianov in 1870 ("Lenin" was a revolutionary pseudonym), came from an intellectual, socially conscious, semiprivileged family. His father was a school inspector, and his mother was the well-educated daughter of a doctor. Lenin was an intelligent and serious youth and became a revolutionary during his first year of university study. Although the execution of his older brother for participating in an assassination plot against Tsar Alexander III may have hardened Lenin's antigovernment attitudes, this was not what made him a revolutionary. He had already begun to develop radical social and political views, partly from intellectual conviction that only fundamental change could right things in Russia and partly from a deep-seated desire to remove injustice and improve the life of the people. By the early 1890s Lenin had become a Marxist and was active in revolutionary circles in St. Petersburg.

What soon distinguished Lenin from hundreds of other Marxist revolutionaries emerging in Russia at that time was his strong will and his devout conviction of both the necessity and possibility of revolution. Lenin's overpowering determination helped him drive ahead regardless of obstacles and setbacks, and it often wore down and swallowed up the resistance of doubting comrades. Lenin possessed many other qualities important to a revolutionary leader, including a powerful personality, a quick and wide-ranging mind, and brilliant political intuition. But when even these failed to win the day for him, he could always fall back on his boundless tenacity; Lenin never gave up on something he really wanted.

And what he wanted most was revolution, first in Russia, then throughout the world. Before the former could be achieved, the working class of Russia had to be roused and educated. Left to its own devices, it would simply develop "trade-union consciousness," a desire only for higher wages and shorter hours. Therefore, Lenin argued, a Marxist party was needed to instill genuine proletarian "class consciousness" in the Russian workers. This accomplished, the party was to guide and lead the workers in revolution and direct the setting up of a dictatorship of the proletariat. Later, in an important addition to Marxism, Lenin declared that the poorer peasants could be enlisted as allies of the workers in this struggle.

"But what sort of party, Comrade Lenin, would be able to do all this?" we can imagine a young Marxist of the early 1900s asking. Lenin's reply, first fully formulated in his tract *What Is to Be Done* published in 1902 and elaborated in practice during the succeeding decade, might have run like this: "First, it must be a small party of dedicated activists. Only people willing to devote all their time and energy to revolutionary work can succeed in indoctrinating, organizing, and leading the proletariat. We have no room for lukewarm sympathizers or revolutionary amateurs. Second, it must be disciplined and centralized. Party members should be free to debate issues but once policy has been decided every member is bound to carry it out vigorously. Finally, the party must be rigorous in defense of its beliefs; it cannot compromise its principles, and particularly it must struggle as un-yieldingly against the bourgeois/capitalist class enemy as against the hated tsarist regime."

This was indeed the sort of party into which Lenin wanted to mold the Bolshevik faction of Russian social democrats. The im-plication that the party alone knew what was best for the masses was made explicit after the Bolsheviks came to power, when Russia was subjected to the dictatorship of the party.

But even with a disciplined elite party, how was revolution possible? Despite Marx's prediction in the 1840s that capitalism would soon collapse, in the early 1900s the capitalist countries of Western Europe seemed stronger than ever; the possibility of proletarian revolution seemed slim indeed. Determined to make a revolution, Lenin had an answer for this as well. In his *Imperial-ism, the Highest Stage of Capitalism*, published in 1915, he argued that the demise of capitalism had been temporarily postponed by the development of finance capitalism—the rule of banks and investment houses—and by the expansion of capitalism overseas. In this phenomenon, called *imperialism*, the financiers were able for a while to prop capitalism up with new profits derived from overseas investments and markets and from exploitation of cheap native labor and raw materials.

Moreover, Lenin maintained that economic expansion led to political control and the rapid division of the non-European world into colonies and spheres of influence of the European powers. But when all the overseas areas had been expropriated, the im-perialist nations, desperate to acquire more, would begin quarrel-ing and would eventually fight among themselves. Thus Lenin saw World War I as an all-out conflict between two groups of imperialists. Because the workers could only lose in such a strug-gle, Lenin urged them to oppose the war and "to turn the im-perialist war into a civil war" of the proletariat against the bour-geoisie in each country. Out of the bitterness, destruction, and chaos of the war Lenin hoped would come a broad workers' revolution in Europe.

But what of the revolution in Russia, his homeland? In principle

Lenin accepted the dominant view of Russian social democracy that Russia must first undergo a bourgeois-democratic revolution—the overthrow of the tsardom—and a capitalist stage of development before a proletarian socialist revolution could take place. In practice, however, Lenin chafed under this timetable and sought to abbreviate the process. As we shall see in Chapter Eight, he was able during 1917 to find a rationale for hastening the proletarian seizure of power in Russia.

Nevertheless, several of the ingredients of that rationale were already part of Lenin's thinking when the February Revolution occurred. First, he pointed out that because the bourgeoisie in Russia was so weak, the working class, though not large or advanced, was in a comparatively strong position, particularly if it could win over the bulk of the peasantry. Second, Lenin believed that the weakness and timidity of the Russian capitalists prevented them from taking the lead in overthrowing tsarism; they would have to be pushed and pulled along in this task by the class-conscious proletariat led by an organized party, the Bolsheviks. Third, the war-weariness, hatred, and misery resulting from the war were creating an explosive revolutionary situation in Russia. Finally, because Russia was backward compared with other imperialist countries, it might be possible to begin the international workers' revolution at this "weak link" in the chain of capitalist states. Touched off in Russia, the proletarian revolution would spread quickly to the more advanced capitalist countries of Western Europe.

With these factors in mind, Lenin, though as surprised as others by the February Revolution, immediately saw it as an opening toward his lifetime goal—a proletarian revolution in Russia directed by the Bolsheviks. In his "Letters from Afar," sent to Russia before he left Switzerland, Lenin declared that the February Revolution meant that the bourgeois-democratic revolution had taken place in Russia, that therefore the workers should be getting ready for the socialist revolution, and that the Bolsheviks should oppose the Provisional government, which was simply an agent of imperialism. He was extremely annoyed at the conciliatory line taken by the Bolsheviks present in Russia during the end of March and the beginning of April and, as we saw above, his first words on reaching Petrograd reflected his militant stance.

Lenin's view of the situation was elaborated shortly after his return in a series of statements known as the April Theses. His three main points were that the workers and the Petrograd Soviet should criticize and contend with the Provisional government, that they should call for and prepare for the transfer of power to the Soviet, and that they should demand an end to the war. At first Lenin's own Bolshevik colleagues were stunned by his radical recommendations, but with his usual doggedness and persuasiveness Lenin soon began to win them over. In early May the Bolshevik party held an all-Russian conference at which Lenin gained a partial victory. While not accepting all of his formulations, the conference nevertheless approved the policies of opposing the Provisional government, demanding peace, and urging fraternization with German soldiers at the front as a revolutionary way of ending the war.

Other Russian politicians considered Lenin either out of touch with the situation or a bit mad. One critical article was labeled, "On the Theses of Lenin, or Why Delirium Is Sometimes Interesting." Neither the leaders of the Provisional government nor the chief figures in the Menshevik and Socialist Revolutionary parties took Lenin too seriously. And there was really little reason why they should. When Lenin returned to Russia the Bolshevik party could count probably no more than 25,000 members in a country of 120 million. Six months later it would be quite a different story.

FREEDOM FOR ALL

The return to political life of prisoners and exiles was a dramatic manifestation of the meaning of liberation. Another, even more basic and widespread, was the revolution's guarantee of civil liberties and the uses to which they were put. First, as one would expect, the political parties applied the new freedoms to their own causes—setting up newspapers and journals, holding meetings and forums, and sending speakers to institutions and enterprises to spread their own particular brand of revolutionary gospel.

But the people as a whole also took to the culture of liberation joyously. Suddenly Russia became one huge debating society. In every office, home, and factory, on every street corner, by every market, people loudly and continuously argued the issues of the day. At once everything was questioned, every authority challenged. Russian society in the spring of 1917 could in part be limned as one immense babble.

Meetings also became a favorite pastime in post-tsarist Russia. As one observer remarked, "If more than two Russians get together, it becomes a meeting." Nothing could be decided without holding a conference at which various points of view could be expressed. So, of course, meetings led to more talk.

In part this stemmed from a sense of relief and exuberance after preceding decades of repression. In part it reflected a determination to enjoy the fruits of the revolution and to participate in furthering it. These attitudes were certainly healthy and constructive for Russian society. But there were other, darker sides to the endless speechifying and assembling. When these activities did not lead to action, when talking and meeting resulted in no concrete improvement in individuals' lives, people became at first frustrated and disappointed, finally angry and resentful. They tended to blame those in authority, and especially the Provisional government, for having failed them and the revolution; they were much more likely to listen to those who promised quick action and definite results—Lenin and the Bolsheviks.

At the same time, the exercise of freedom by Russians after the revolution was so intense and so complete that it soon bordered on anarchy. Issues not only had to be talked out and conferred on, decisions were not only to be challenged and reviewed; they had to be acted on. But in fact instructions were not carried out, policies were not followed, and little could actually be accomplished. To many people the revolution meant that no one could tell them any longer what they had to do, whether the authority was a landlord, factory owner, bureaucrat, teacher, or whoever. In short, liberation came to signify not just a throwing off of old unjust tsarist restraints but of all restraints. As we shall see shortly, it also meant striving to satisfy one's own needs and wants, regardless of the interests of others.

Finally, and perhaps most important in my view, the enthusiasm with which the Russian people embraced the freedoms that followed the February Revolution masked several deep-rooted emotions. One was hatred of the old order and the upper classes; the enjoyment of liberty was a way of compensating for the humiliations of the past, a way of defying the old values and relationships. To be sure, during the first months of the revolution liberation was applied in a good-natured, almost friendly manner. But as conditions worsened and the hoped-for gains failed to materialize, popular attitudes became more bitter, cynical, and hostile. This undoubtedly paved the way for the savagery and hatred that marked so many episodes in the civil war of 1918–1921.

Freedom also led to fear and insecurity, powerful emotions in determining the attitudes and actions of the masses. In 1917 Russians entered a new world, one about which most of them knew nothing. They were uncertain what to expect, not sure how to act, puzzled as to what to do. In many ways it was a frightening world. Old beliefs, customs, and ties were swept away. They had no training or preparation for citizenship or liberty. They had been nurtured in an ordered and authoritarian society in which village elders, owners, priests, officials, and the tsar had told them how to behave and what to do. Now the disorientation begun by modernization and intensified by the war was almost complete. It was a bewildering prospect, and many groped for clear directives and firm signs.

Beyond apprehension of the novel and unknown was an even greater fear—the fear of counterrevolution. For almost everyone in Russia the revolution came to symbolize their strongest aspirations and brightest dreams. The revolution meant different things to different individuals, but almost all embraced it as the key to a better life, for themselves personally and for society. People were terrified that this great hope of hopes might be snatched away. Because of this and because of the underlying current of hatred for the old regime and the old ruling classes, the specter of counter-revolution became the single most important element in the popular and political psychology of the revolutionary months of 1917.

REVOLUTIONARY HOPES

Besides freedom for all, the February Revolution gave key elements in Russian society a chance to fulfill their specific aspirations. The largest groups cut across the political parties; though they were not organized as interest groups and were seldom thoroughly self-conscious, we can see in retrospect that these broad groups had particular goals and an elemental determination to achieve them. Moreover, thanks to the pioneering effort of Marc Ferro, a French historian who by chance was able to examine letters, telegrams, and petitions addressed from individuals and groups throughout Russia to the Petrograd Soviet and the Provisional government in the first few months after the February Revolution, we have a fairly clear picture of what the people of Russia wanted from the revolution.[1] The four most important groups were the workers, the peasants, the soldiers, and the national minorities of Russia.

The workers were primarily interested in economic issues and betterment of their working and living conditions. They wanted an eight-hour workday, higher wages, protection against arbitrary discipline in the factory and against employer lockouts, improved vacation and pension arrangements, and some say in determining job classifications and wage rates. They also wanted better housing and improved sanitation. As one workers' petition declared:

At the factory there is no medical aid . . . No usable washbowls, if there were any, no boiling water or even warm water,

[1] Marc Ferro, *The Russian Revolution of February 1917,* trans. J. L. Richards (Englewood Cliffs, N.J., 1972).

the toilets broken since 1915. . . . Fines are showered on the workers without their knowing what they are for.[2]

They were at first little interested in political issues or workers' participation in management. Only later, when their demands were not met and factory owners resorted to lockouts, did the workers begin to take over the plants and to adopt a radical political stance.

The peasants had one overriding passion—more land. As one popular saying put it, "When we take the land from the Kulaks [rich peasants], it's Anarchy. When they take our sons, it's Patriotism."[3] The peasants had some secondary concerns, but land was what they had their hearts set on, and before long they began to act to make this dream come true. As we shall see in Chapter Four, they simply took the land.

The soldiers' main goal was not peace—at least not at first. In fact, none of the groups demanded an end to the war in the beginning. Some even submitted to Petrograd patriotic pledges of support for the war effort. Later this was to change. But right after the February Revolution the soldiers wanted chiefly a reform of internal army life. They objected strenuously to the humiliating conditions under which they had to serve. One soldiers' committee demanded:

1. Improved pay . . . which will show the government's interest in the army, thereby encouraging it and reinforcing the defense of free Russia.

   To increase allotments for soldiers' families and to insure them against the loss of the capacity to work . . . An army assured of the well being of its dependents can devote itself to the fight against the enemy.

   To give certain guarantees to the soldiers who will have become disabled because of the war.

2. Certain functions should be performed by means of elections.

[2] *Ibid.,* p. 113.
[3] *Ibid.,* p. 123.

3. The improvement of the soldier's lot, especially in the matter of sanitation.

4. The abolition of military salute and the practice of coming to attention.

5. The forbidding of discussion of political problems in the army, as proposed by the officers' committee, would be a return to the old regime.[4]

Shortly we shall see what impact the soldiers' aspirations had on the course of the war and of the revolution.

The last group to assert its own interests in this period were the non-Russian peoples of the old empire. Their claims varied from full independence espoused by the more extreme factions to cultural autonomy in a Russian state. For example, the Rada (council) of the Ukraine declared:

> The happy day is here when the Ukraine, enslaved for centuries, begins a new life. . . . Get ready for the National Constituent Assembly where the voice of the great Ukrainian people must resound united to defend the autonomy of our native land and the formation of a federal state.[5]

The revolutionary hopes of these major groups in Russian society had two important characteristics in common: (1) each group was pursuing its own self-interest with little regard for the needs or aspirations of the others or for the welfare of the society as a whole; and (2) at the outset the groups were all cheerfully confident that their claims would soon be met. They appeared blithely unaware of the difficulties that might prevent their getting what they wanted. Thus when their hopes remained largely unfulfilled, they quickly became frustrated and resentful. They were more than ready to listen to anyone who promised to make their dreams come true.

[4] *Ibid.*, p. 133.
[5] *Ibid.*, p. 146.

Table 3.   ASPIRATIONS OF IMPORTANT GROUPS IN RUSSIA

Spring 1917

Workers	*Peasants*	*Soldiers*	*National Minorities*
eight-hour workday	land	improved pay	self-determination
higher wages	lower prices for town goods	better benefits	cultural identity
better benefits		better living conditions	autonomy
improved sanitation and housing	higher prices for farm goods	end of arbitrary discipline	
grievance procedures	lower taxes	end of humiliating treatment by officers	
		civil and political rights	

Added in Summer and Fall 1917

peace	peace	peace	peace
workers' control of factories	local self-government	elected committees	independence
reliable food supply		demobilization	
"all power to the Soviets"			

THE LIBERALS' PRINCIPLES

As Monday morning quarterbacks, we can easily look back and see what the leaders of Russia's moderate Provisional government should have done—make peace, give the land to the peasants, help the workers, free the national minorities. But could they? In light of their beliefs, the behavior of the liberals in 1917 was consistent and logical. But, of course, they were acting in an elemental and illogical situation. A major tragedy of the Russian Revolution is certainly the steadfast devotion of its liberal protagonists to such noble ideals as freedom, democracy, self-determination, and honor—an entirely praiseworthy devotion that could end only in their own defeat and the assured destruction of the very principles they were defending.

A fundamental tenet of the liberal position was that, voiceless for centuries, the Russian people as a whole should now have the final say on the basic issues of their own future, from the structure of the new state to central economic and social policies. In principle this position could hardly be faulted, not by the Russian people nor even by the Bolsheviks, who grudgingly supported it. But in the wartime disorder, revolutionary uncertainty, and age-old backwardness that characterized Russian life in 1917, having the citizenry express its will was not so easy. As we saw earlier, the liberals believed that they must first convoke a Constituent Assembly, which could decide on the future state system, set up a representative government, and counsel on basic policies. This was to be elected by universal suffrage, and an electoral commission was soon formed to prepare for the vote. Since the difficulties of determining eligibility, registering voters, and arranging for balloting throughout the length and breadth of Russia were immense, the elections had to be put off again and again. Pressure from the government could perhaps have speeded up the process but not a great deal.

The intent was laudable, the procedures correct, if slow, and the result disastrous. Workers, peasants, and other groups were in no mood to wait; they expected the revolution to solve their problems at once. By the time elections to the Constituent Assembly were held, the Bolsheviks had already come to power on a wave of popular radicalism, and they soon dissolved the assembly. Yet should the liberals have decided key issues on their own, without consulting the people? This would have violated their lifelong belief in representative government and destroyed a major principle for which the revolution had been fought.

An interesting example of how trying to put this basic tenet into practice created great difficulties for the liberals was the question of the non-Russian nationalities. Even though some liberals personally favored retaining the bulk of the old Russian Empire in a unitary state, most of them acknowledged the right of national self-determination. But they believed that the Provisional government could not grant permanent concessions to the non-Russians for two reasons. First, since groups representing the minorities were largely self-appointed, a mechanism for ascertaining the will of, say, the Ukrainian people had to be established. Second, however, once the wishes of the Ukrainians had been determined, their desires had to be considered in the light of the will of the Russian citizenry as a whole acting through a Constituent Assembly representing all the peoples of the empire. The liberals were convinced that they had no right to parcel out the patrimony of the Russian people without their consent.

The Provisional government took a basically centralist position for practical reasons as well. Its leaders did not want to disrupt the war effort by letting groups on Russia's borders establish autonomy or independence. They were concerned that such concessions to the minorities would result in a federal system that was likely to be politically ineffective. And they feared that ceding too much to the national minorities would weaken the centralized Russian economy. But their basic objection was still one of principle.

Another example of how adherence to principle blocked needed political action was land reform. The peasants made it abundantly clear that they wanted to divide the land. The Provisional government decided it could not do this, first because simply to take the land from its present owners, whether the state or private persons, and give it to the peasants violated the right of private property, in which the liberals deeply believed. Second, however, both liberals and moderate socialists opposed immediate distribution of the land because only the Constituent Assembly could resolve such a basic issue as the future agricultural system of the country—whether land was to be nationalized, as the socialists desired, or held privately, as the liberals preferred. These were undoubtedly logical positions, but needless to say they meant nothing to the peasants, who went ahead and seized the land.

Civil liberties was another area in which both moderate socialist and liberal leaders of the revolution stuck admirably to their principles—at considerable cost. Determined to protect freedom of speech, press, and assembly, horror-stricken at the thought of imitating the repressive ways of the hated tsarist government, they refused to take forceful action against the Bolsheviks, even when it became obvious that the latter intended to overthrow the Provisional government and shoulder aside the liberal and moderate socialist parties. To pleas that they clap the Bolshevik leaders in jail and shut down Bolshevik newspapers and publishing houses, the liberals and moderate socialists responded—quite correctly—that such action would destroy the revolution in an attempt to save it. In June 1917, after an abortive Bolshevik demonstration in Petrograd, I. G. Tsereteli, a prominent Menshevik and minister of communications in the Provisional government, pleaded with his colleagues to disarm the Bolsheviks, by force if necessary. But several ministers and fellow socialists overrode his proposal, arguing that repressive action would be a mistake and that the government should not attack fellow revolutionaries.[6]

On the crucial issue of the war the liberals were not entirely consistent, for one set of their beliefs came into conflict with and overrode another. If they had been faithful to their principle of not acting on major policy matters without the consent of the people, they should have demanded that the Provisional government not continue the war without some sort of popular referendum. But in practical terms a referendum was difficult to arrange, and the Germans in any case were not about to suspend military operations while the Russian citizenry decided whether to continue to fight.

Moreover, other principles strongly dictated to the liberals that

[6] I. G. Tsereteli, *Vospominaniia o Fevral'skoi Revoliutsii* (Paris, 1963), II, pp. 227–228.

Russia had to remain in the war. The most compelling was patriotism and loyalty to the Motherland. In retrospect it is difficult to understand how the combatants in World War I, and especially the Russians, could have wanted to continue to fight after years of slaughter and destruction. It defies reason; but of course it was not reasonable. All the belligerent populations were governed by irrational emotions, loyalties, and hatreds the intensity of which is almost impossible to recover. We can now see that it was madness for Russia to stay in the war. But at the time people could only see that to leave the war meant either to surrender to the "Huns" and see German military hordes occupy Mother Russia, or to be forced to accept a humiliating peace in which Russia would have to give up all the goals for which it already had sacrificed so much.

Besides fervent nationalism and love of country, other principles were at work in support of Russia's remaining in the war. After the February Revolution and the entry of the United States into the war, the Allied cause became a sacred one—a moral struggle against German militarism, a crusade "to make the world safe for democracy." Russian liberals as much as anyone were befogged by this rhetoric. To withdraw from the war would betray the liberal world that they had always revered. It would mean abandoning the liberal principles on which they had been nurtured and to the achievement of which their lives had been dedicated.

Finally, there was the issue of Russia's commitments. For some this meant the postwar territorial gains that Russia had been promised in the secret treaties negotiated among the Allies in 1915–1916, particularly control of the Turkish Straits and Constantinople. From our perspective this concern may seem like pure acquisitiveness, but at the time many Russians saw expansion as essential to protect Russia's national interests and as just compensation for the terrible hardships and burdens the war had imposed on the Russian people. But even for those liberals and moderate socialists who wanted to publish the secret treaties and who repudiated the idea of financial or territorial gains from the war, there remained the issue of Russia's integrity—its solemn undertaking to support the French and British (and now American) peoples in their struggle against Germany. As the Kadet party put it in an appeal to the people on May 4: "Can free Russia betray the noble peoples of the West, who supported us at the most difficult times?"

In fact, no Russian leaders except Lenin demanded an end to the war, and neither in the first few months of the revolution did the Russian people. There is little doubt, however, that if somehow the Provisional government could have gotten out of the war, the story of 1917 would have been entirely different. But even if there had been a practical way to withdraw, on principle the government could not do so.

THE ARMY, THE WAR, AND ORDER NO. 1

General attitudes toward the war remain a puzzling aspect of the situation in Russia in the spring of 1917. It is clear that at heart almost every Russian was sick of the war. Yet publicly almost everyone supported it, and many welcomed the revolution primarily as a way of reviving and bolstering the war effort. This divergence between people's elemental feelings and their public attitudes can only be explained by the powerful grip of patriotism on everyone's mind and emotions.

The reaction of the army high command to the revolution was one of tempered enthusiasm. Most of the generals were happy to see the end of the inept tsarist regime and hoped for a more vigorous and efficient prosecution of the war under the new government. At the same time, they regretted the loss of the traditions, class mores, and stability they associated with tsarism, and they feared the social changes and the uncertain future that the revolution seemed to promise. As we saw earlier, the high command did not intervene directly in the political events of the revolution, maintaining the traditional stance that the army should stay out of politics.

The generals and commanders of the Russian army were aware

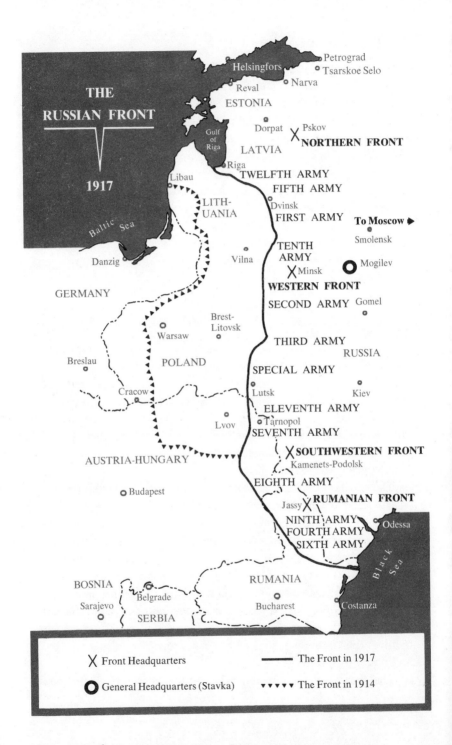

that their troops were war-weary and exhausted, but they hoped the revolution might revive the soldiers' flagging spirits. They recognized that reforms within the army were necessary but were divided on what these should be and how far they should go.

Most of the officers shared the attitudes of their superiors, but there were some differences of opinion among the junior grades. Few officers at the lower levels were part of the prewar officer caste. They had been elevated from the ranks or hastily recruited during the war. Some had clear-cut political views, from moderate to radical, and many were quite critical of existing conditions in the army and sympathized with the soldiers' demands for reform. Moreover, a number of younger officers believed that the war could be continued and the soldiers persuaded to fight effectively only if the army were democratized.

We have already seen what the soldiers' chief complaints were, revolving around too-harsh discipline and treatment as inferiors. Since the soldiers had played a considerable role in the February Revolution in Petrograd and were partners with workers in the Petrograd Soviet, it is not surprising that one of the first concrete results of the revolution was army reform. On March 14 the Soviet issued its famous Order No. 1 to the soldiers and sailors of Petrograd. Whether this marked the beginning of the end for the Russian army is a matter of controversy.

Actually Order No. 1 was a compromise. Radical soldiers in the Soviet were demanding that enlisted men elect all officers, but the Soviet executive committee was unwilling to go that far. Order No. 1 had three main objectives. The first was to ameliorate the harsh conditions of life for the average soldier. Some of the most offensive tsarist army regulations were abolished; for example, off-duty soldiers no longer had to come to attention and salute officers, the ordinary Russian soldier no longer had to address his officers as "Your Excellency" or "Your Honor," and officers were forbidden to use the familiar form of the verb, a mark of condescension, in addressing soldiers. Disciplinary codes were to be reviewed, and soldiers were guaranteed full civil and political rights.

Second, Order No. 1 provided for the election of soldiers' committees in each company, battalion, regiment, and division. These committees were to represent the interests of the soldiers on all matters except actual military operations. Not surprisingly, this reform was highly controversial, just as it would be in the American army today. Some of the committees were composed of bright, cooperative individuals who worked hard to advance the welfare both of their fellows and of the unit as a whole. Other committees were quarrelsome and troublesome, completely disrupting the ability of the given unit to function effectively. A few officers, recognizing that the soldiers often elected popular officers to the soldiers' committees and that the committees might improve the morale and efficiency of the men, cooperated with them wholeheartedly. Many officers either dragged their feet or tried to ignore the committees. A few officers who resisted the committees entirely, especially those with German names, were beaten or killed by enraged mobs of soldiers.

Finally, Order No. 1 provided that no Petrograd garrison troops could be transferred outside the city without the authorization of the Soviet. This confirmed what the Provisional government had promised upon taking office, but it removed a fundamental prerogative of the army command and the government. Nevertheless it was a key provision for the Petrograd soldiers, who did not want to be transferred to the front and who insisted that they had to remain in the capital to defend the revolution from counterrevolution.

Order No. 1 asserted far-reaching authority for the Petrograd Soviet but the Provisional government, aware of the strength of the soldiers' bloc in the Soviet and in the city, could not reject this sweeping claim. After trying in vain to persuade the Soviet to withdraw or soften Order No. 1, the ministers of the Provisional government decided to incorporate some of its provisions in a Declaration of Soldiers' Rights, which the Soviet also approved. Later, in an effort to raise morale, head off mutiny, and restore authority throughout the army, the government and the high command endorsed the formation of elected soldiers' committees in all units. Before long these committees became linked to the nationwide system of soviets, and "dual power" existed not only in the government but in the army as well.

By early May 1917, two months after the collapse of the tsarist regime, life in Russia seemed to be settling down. The surprise and shock of the sudden disappearance of the old order had worn off. The euphoria which had greeted the February Revolution had simmered down to a cheery optimism, though the uncertainties of the future brought occasional qualms. A newspaper column of May 4 commented:

> The present moment places before us strictly limited and comparatively circumscribed tasks. The Provisional Government fulfills *these* tasks completely honestly and conscientiously, but it can solve them only with the unanimous support of the public, in an atmosphere of general good will. Without confidence, there can be neither authority nor firm power. . . . Because of the extreme seriousness of the situation, it is necessary to forget controversies as much as possible and unite around the Provisional Government to make it really strong. Without this, we risk losing all the attainments of the revolution.[7]

Most Russians were still drinking thirstily at the font of unaccustomed freedom. Politicians, whether of the old Duma, long underground, released prisoners, or returned exiles, were happily declaiming, negotiating, and arguing. Journalists and writers spilled out an endless flow of words in newspapers, journals, and books. And Russians everywhere talked and met, convened and debated, happy to be liberated and determined not to lose what they had gained.

Each group had its own revolutionary dreams and began to press its aspirations on the authorities, whether Soviet or governmental. Few thought realistically about what their demands meant

[7] From *Russkia vedomosti,* no. 88, April 21, 1917 (old style), p. 3; cited in Robert Paul Browder and Alexander F. Kerensky (eds.), *The Russian Provisional Government 1917: Documents* (Stanford, Calif., 1961), III, pp. 1233–1234.

or whether they could be realized. All counted on the miracle of the revolution to usher in a golden era in their lives.

The liberals, firm in their constitutional and libertarian principles and committed to the war, struggled to make the new order work. But a reformed army, a free people, a democratic government weighed little against the massive economic, social, and managerial problems that wartime Russia still faced.

4
The Radicalization of Russia
★

For two days in mid-July crowds surged over the main boulevards of Petrograd. Excited, angry, and determined, the demonstrators knew what they were against—the war and the Provisional government. They were less clear about what they favored. At one point on July 17 a mob dragged Victor Chernov, a Soviet leader and minister of agriculture in the Provisional government, into a car. He could easily have been beaten or killed but for the timely intervention of Leon Trotsky, by then a leading Bolshevik and a prominent radical figure in the Petrograd Soviet. After Trotsky had harangued the unruly crowd, Chernov was released and permitted to return to the Soviet offices.

That same day, on another occasion, Chernov was reportedly trying to calm a group of demonstrators by explaining that since the revolution was in a bourgeois-democratic phase, it was not appropriate for the socialist parties in the Soviet to take over the government. Finally, an outraged worker shook his fist at Chernov and bawled, "Take power, you son-of-a-bitch, when they give it to you!"

This situation and the attitude of the crowds differed greatly from the circumstances and popular behavior during the February

Revolution only four months earlier. Why was there such elemental dissatisfaction with the Provisional government, which
everyone had either supported or tolerated only a short time
before? What had happened to radicalize the masses?

"DOWN WITH THE WAR!"

As spring turned into summer in 1917, the people's latent war-
weariness and pacifism began to surface. Public support for the
war dwindled rapidly, and by midsummer had almost disappeared.
The course of events between late April and early August revealed
how far antiwar feeling had progressed.

In Chapter Two we saw that in late March the Provisional government and the Petrograd Soviet had finally reached tenuous
agreement jointly to support the war and to seek a revision of war
aims. But important leaders in both camps believed this an unsatis-
factory compromise. Professor Paul N. Miliukov, head of the
Kadet party and minister of foreign affairs, feared that any revision of war aims might endanger Allied promises of Russian
control of the Turkish Straits, which for him was Russia's most
important goal in the war. On the other hand, radical spokesmen
in the Soviet wanted the new government to repudiate any imperialist agreements, declare new war aims based on no annexations and no indemnities, and persuade France and Britain to
join Russia in peace negotiations with Germany and Austria.

These disparate points of view created an atmosphere of suspicion and friction. Finally, the cabinet of the Provisional government, in an effort to allay the fears of Soviet leaders, offered to
transmit formally to the Allied nations the Provisional government's public declaration to the people of Russia of April 9, which
specifically renounced any imperialist goals. Miliukov agreed to
do this, but insisted on sending with the declaration an explana-
tory note, which the cabinet approved. When the note was made
public on May 3, however, a great hullabaloo arose.

What created the stir was not so much what the note said as
its general tone and that Miliukov, who to many had become a

symbol of imperialist aspirations, had written it. The note claimed that the Russian people's zest for victory was greater than ever and promised that the Provisional government would "fully observe the obligations that were undertaken in regard to our Allies"—which, of course, for Miliukov, included the secret treaties and the promise to Russia of the Turkish Straits. By that afternoon soldiers from several regiments were on the streets demonstrating and shouting, "Down with Miliukov!" Representatives of the Soviet addressed the demonstrators and persuaded most of them to return to barracks. That evening leaders of the Soviet and of the government agreed that to mollify radical sentiment in the Soviet the government would issue a public explanation of ambiguous passages in the note to the Allies.

But the next day the demonstrations continued, with large numbers of workers joining the soldiers. Groups organized by the Kadet party in support of Miliukov also appeared in the streets, and some clashes occurred. Several people were killed and a score or so injured. Banners now appeared saying, "DOWN WITH THE WAR!" "DOWN WITH THE PROVISIONAL GOVERNMENT!" On the evening of May 4 the crowds dispersed, although the political crisis persisted for ten more days. In retrospect we can see that the May events contained several significant portents.

For the first time in the revolution widespread opposition to the war had been openly displayed. It was a clear indication that patriotic slogans and appeals could no longer contain popular revulsion against the war. In addition, the May crisis foreshadowed the growing divergence between the position of the moderate socialists in the Soviet and the attitudes and demands of the Petrograd masses. At one point during the disorders when a Soviet leader attempted to persuade a group of demonstrators to go home, they in effect told him to mind his own business, they knew what they were doing.

Finally, the crisis demonstrated the fundamental weakness of the Provisional government and the considerable power of the Soviet. Not only did the cabinet have to request the Soviet to work out a solution to the situation, but the government, it turned out, could not control military units in the capital that were officially under its authority. On May 4 General L. G. Kornilov, who later headed a counterrevolutionary movement but who was then commander of the Petrograd military district, ordered troops to quell the unrest. The units involved asked the Soviet what they should do. Leaders of the Soviet persuaded Kornilov that such action would only exacerbate the situation, and he rescinded his orders, but requested to be transferred from Petrograd. A reorganized Provisional government survived the May crisis, but obviously it did not have full authority over either the citizenry or its own nominal forces.

In the aftermath of the crisis Miliukov was forced to resign, and in an effort to bolster the government, some of the liberals decided to ask socialist leaders from the Soviet to enter the cabinet. To the radical members of the Soviet it seemed like treason to join the bourgeoisie in ruling the country. But after hesitating for a few days the leaders of the Menshevik and Socialist Revolutionary parties, who were a majority in the Soviet, decided to accept the offer to form a coalition government. They rationalized their decision in two ways. First, they maintained on patriotic grounds that having socialist members of the Soviet in the government would strengthen the war effort by broadening popular support for the government's policies. Second, they argued on ideological grounds that although the revolution was still in its bourgeois-democratic phase, socialists had an obligation to push that revolution forward rapidly and to ensure that it was as democratic and free as possible. This obligation could best be met at the present moment by entering a coalition cabinet with the representatives of the bourgeoisie.

Though appearing to make sense at the time, this decision was ultimately fatal to the interests of the moderate socialists. In reality and in the popular mind it linked them inextricably with the policies and actions of the government. Thus they were soon tarnished by the government's sins of both commission and omission. The socialists were blamed not only for what the people felt the government did wrong but also for the government's con-

Alexander Kerensky, revolutionary romantic and prime minister of the Russian Provisional Government in the summer of 1917, strolling in the gardens of the deposed tsar's summer palace of Tsarskoeselo. *Popperfoto*

tinuing inability to meet the masses' revolutionary hopes. On the other hand, the new arrangement left the Bolsheviks free of responsibility, able to castigate both the government and the moderate socialists and to promise the people what they wanted.

The new coalition cabinet of the Provisional government contained ten liberal or "capitalist" ministers and six socialists, including two Mensheviks and two Socialist Revolutionaries. Prince Lvov remained premier but the chief figure in the cabinet, and in all subsequent ones, was Alexander F. Kerensky, a radical lawyer of vaguely socialist views who had made something of a reputation as an orator in the Fourth Duma and who had entered the original cabinet of the Provisional government, not as a representative of the Petrograd Soviet, to which he belonged, but as an individual. Kerensky now became minister of war and energetically set about readying the country for new war efforts.

On May 19 the reorganized government issued a statement of policy, endorsed by the Soviet, that called for "the speediest achievement of a general peace . . . a peace without annexations or indemnities, on the basis of self-determination of peoples." It also promised preparations for renegotiating war aims with the Allies and "the strengthening of democratic principles" in the army. But neither the reshuffling of the government nor the affirmation of a clearer policy toward the war and toward army reform was able to arrest the rapid escalation of antiwar sentiment among the population and the growing pressure for some radical step to end the conflict.

KERENSKY AND THE JULY OFFENSIVE

The anomalous situation of a broadened and presumably more popular government's pursuing a war that fewer and fewer people supported might have dragged on for many months but for the decision of the new cabinet finally to launch a military offensive against the Germans and Austrians. The offensive had been under discussion since late in 1916, when the Allies had persuaded the Russians to accept a strategic war plan for 1917 in which the Russians were committed to a major offensive on the Eastern Front as a means of relieving German pressure on the Allies along the Western Front. The timing of the offensive was left open after the Russians pointed out that they would need a considerable period to organize and supply such a large-scale undertaking. After the February Revolution the offensive became an increasingly urgent issue for the Provisional government for two reasons.

On the Allied side, the French and British found themselves in a desperate situation on the Western Front in the spring of 1917. With the first American troops not expected to arrive in Europe for some months, the Germans launched a major attack, which soon drove the Allies back toward Paris. Pointing to the mortal danger they were in, the French and British put tremendous pressure on the new Russian government to launch an offensive in the East as soon as possible. On the Russian side, a number of generals, most of the liberals, and some of the moderate socialists somehow convinced themselves that a successful offensive might bring a quick victory and prove to be a panacea for their problems. They came to believe that it would restore discipline and stem the disintegration of the army, bolster the population's sagging spirits, and garner confidence and widespread support for the government. The conviction that the offensive would be successful despite the demoralization of the troops and that more fighting would lead to the calming of the war-weary masses only demonstrates how patriotic fervor and wartime emotions can warp the judgments and distort the common sense of usually reasonable people. Typical of the extravagant but misguided hopes placed in the offensive was the statement by a conservative Kadet that "If we succeed in launching an offensive . . . then Russia's cure will be quick and complete."

Although several army commanders reported that their troops were in no condition to undertake an offensive, the general staff and the government agreed to launch one in early July. Kerensky made it his principal task to oversee its preparation and to rally the troops and the public behind it. Though abused by Soviet historians as a tool of the capitalist oppressors, blamed by conservative writers for letting the Bolsheviks come to power, and scorned by many Western observers as posturing and ineffectual, Kerensky had many qualities that fitted him to inspire one last effort in the war and that in less turbulent times might have made him a successful leader. Only thirty-six years old, he was energetic, ambitious, a persuasive speaker, and fervently idealistic. Passionately committed to both the revolution and the war, Kerensky for a brief interval was able to rouse the Russian people and the front-line soldiers to back the offensive, although, or perhaps because, as this sample suggests, his rhetoric was a bit overblown:

All of you, warriors of liberated Russia, from soldier to general, all of you fulfill the hard but glorious duty of defending revolutionary Russia. Do not only remember this duty of yours. But by defending Russia you are fighting also for the triumph of the lofty ideals of our revolution, for liberty, equality, and fraternity. Not a single drop of blood will be shed for a wrong cause. It is not for the sake of conquest and violence but for the sake of saving free Russia that you will go forward where your commanders and the Government lead you. It is impossible to expel the enemy by standing still. On the points of your bayonets you will bring peace, right, truth, and justice. Free sons of Russia, you will move forward in serried ranks, united by the discipline of duty and by your supreme love for the revolution and your homeland.[1]

Yet his style was dynamic, and even thirty years later, when I heard Kerensky (then living in the United States) speak, he could still excite interest and stir emotions.

Numerous eyewitnesses attest to Kerensky's ability to win over even hostile audiences. On one occasion in Moscow ladies in the crowd took off their jewelry and threw it onstage in response to Kerensky's appeal for concrete support for the war effort. A number of times sullen, dispirited troops were turned into cheering, enthusiastic supporters of the offensive by one of Kerensky's stem-

[1] From Kerensky's Order of the Day on becoming minister of war, May 27, 1917, in Robert Paul Browder and Alexander F. Kerensky (eds.), *The Russian Provisional Government 1917: Documents* (Stanford, Calif., 1961), II, p. 936.

winding perorations, so much so that he was soon dubbed "persuader-in-chief" of the army.

In its first few days the Russian army's July offensive was quite successful, particularly along the southern part of the front against the Austrians. But then German reserve shock troops were brought up and a counterattack began. Once the offensive had been turned back, it soon turned into a rout, despite orders (sometimes obeyed) for officers and rear units to shoot deserters and those retreating pell-mell. The failure of the offensive meant that the Provisional government could not hope to solve its problems and redeem its weakening position by victory on the battlefield. Undoubtedly that had been a vain hope from the beginning, but it had sustained many moderates up to that point. Now the future looked bleak.

The failure of the July offensive also signaled the practical end of the war as an issue in the revolution. The government and the Allies continued to talk about reorganizing and resurrecting the Russian war effort, but it was meaningless talk. In the army the death penalty for desertion and mutiny was restored for a time, but it had little effect and served mainly to heighten resentment, thereby further undermining discipline and contributing to rebellious sentiment. Conservatives and some high army officers tried to support a seizure of power by General Kornilov aimed at suppressing the radicals at home and reviving the army's fighting capacity at the front, but it failed ignominiously, as we shall see shortly. Moreover, throughout the succeeding weeks of the revolution the soldiers deserted in ever-increasing numbers and the people as a whole simply stopped caring about the war. With an estimated 700,000 desertions between July and October, the army melted away and was useless as an effective military force. In the cities and villages people's chief concern was peace—indeed, peace at any price.

THE SOVIETS

The soviets formed in the Revolution of 1905 had been popular and quite successful as revolutionary organs. Lenin in particular had noted their suitability as a mechanism for representing and channeling revolutionary power. Among all shades of socialists and within articulate working-class circles the memory and reputation of the soviets were favorable. Thus when the Petrograd Soviet was resurrected in March 1917 as the Soviet of Workers' and Soldiers' Deputies, it could draw upon a reservoir of goodwill and faith, and it benefited from positive popular attitudes toward it. This helps explain why, despite its meager record of achievement, the prestige and power of the Petrograd Soviet continued to grow during the revolution and why the institution of soviets spread.

Several other factors nurtured the burgeoning soviet movement. The soviet was a familiar institution for peasants and other lower-class Russians with a peasant background (which included almost everyone) since it may have been modeled on, and certainly resembled in significant ways, the traditional village or communal assembly. Moreover, the soviet corresponded closely to the spirit of the times and the mood of the masses. It was revolutionary and democratic; it gave people a chance to air their views and complaints; and it represented quite accurately the interests and aspirations of the people. Finally, the soviet was really without competition; it was the only body with which the masses could identify. The government seemed alien and symbolic of the upper classes; the socialist parties were too ideological and quarrelsome; and trade unions and similar institutions appeared too narrow and particular.

It is therefore hardly surprising that soviets spread rapidly all over Russia and that soviets of peasants' deputies soon emerged alongside those for workers and soldiers. By the end of March, soviets existed in most of the major cities of European Russia, and by the end of April, in many of the villages of the empire. On April 11 an All-Russian Conference of Soviets was held in Petrograd. It brought together representatives from 138 local soviets and from some 45 military soviets. The conference urged formation of new soviets and establishment of links with peasant organizations. It also added provincial representatives to the executive committee of the Petrograd Soviet, making it an all-Russian body.

Although the Petrograd Soviet and executive committee had the greatest prestige and authority, provincial soviets and peasant soviets and committees played a significant role in the unfolding of the revolution, as the historian John Keep has shown.[2] These institutions largely excluded the middle class and basically represented nonpropertied groups in Russian society. They were primarily concerned with local interests and were antigovernment and anticentralist in their orientation, which weakened the ability of the Provisional government to exert more than nominal authority over the country. In many areas the populace looked to the soviet rather than to the government for its needs and as a source of power. Finally, because of their link with Petrograd, the local soviets brought the increasingly mutinous countryside and the revolutionary capital closer, making a counterrevolutionary movement based in the provinces less likely.

Some local soviets dominated daily life in their districts. For example, the soviet in Kronstadt, the naval base and industrial town on an island near Petrograd, tolerated the presence of a representative of the Provisional government but itself actually governed the island. The soviet in the Siberian town of Krasnoyarsk rationed food and goods and approved the transfer of local factories to trade unions. Peasant soviets and committees often ignored representatives of the central government and took into their own hands both local affairs and the confiscation and distribution of land.

Because of the rapid spread of soviets it was possible to convene an All-Russian Congress of Soviets as early as June 16. As in the Petrograd Soviet and in most local soviets, the Bolsheviks were a small minority at this congress. Of 777 delegates who declared their party allegiance, only 105 were Bolsheviks, while there were 285 Socialist Revolutionaries (SRs) and 248 Mensheviks. Yet to some extent this ratio of party representation was misleading. The masses were in fact becoming increasingly radical, although not yet pro-Bolshevik. This was partly because the Bolshevik position was not widely known outside of some urban workers' circles and

[2] John Keep, *The Russian Revolution: A Study in Mass Mobilization* (New York, 1976).

certain units of the Petrograd garrison. It was also because soldiers were disproportionately represented in both the Petrograd Soviet and the Congress of Soviets. In Petrograd every military unit (usually a company of 250 men) could elect a representative to the Soviet, while there was only 1 delegate per 1,000 workers; thus some 160,000 soldiers had as many representatives as some 400,000 workers. The soldiers, predominantly peasants, tended at this point to support the vague revolutionary socialism of the SRs rather than the tough Marxist argumentation of the Bolsheviks.

Nevertheless, a significant sign of the leftward sweep of the revolution occurred shortly before the Congress of Soviets met, when the Workers' Section of the Petrograd Soviet passed by 173 to 144 a Bolshevik-sponsored resolution calling for the transfer of power to the soviets. The Bolsheviks did not win control of the whole Soviet until three months later, but this early victory suggested that they were more closely attuned to the increasingly radical feelings of the people than were the other parties.

At the congress Lenin advanced the slogan "All Power to the Soviets," denounced the new government of liberals and moderate socialists as a group of imperialist profiteers, and called for an end to the war through revolutionary action. Naturally the congress did not endorse Lenin's radical platform, but its sessions did provide a useful forum for propagandizing the Bolshevik position. Before closing, the congress declared its confidence in the new government by the resounding vote of 543 to 126 with 52 abstentions.

THE REVOLUTION FROM BELOW

In external appearances, then, things seemed to be going well for the Provisional government. Warmly endorsed by the voices of revolutionary democracy in the Petrograd Soviet, encouraged morally and financially by the Allies, preparing a major offensive on the Eastern Front, the ministers of the new cabinet might well have been sanguine. But in fact, beneath the surface, the revolutionary crisis was deepening and the Russian people were becoming more radical with each passing day.

What led to the more revolutionary mood of the masses? Revulsion against the war was clearly one factor; burdened by defeat, bitter over heavy sacrifices that seemed pointless, Russians saw no reason to go on fighting. Another element was the revolutionary psychology of the times. As we saw in Chapter Three, the people understood the revolution to mean their liberation not only from past oppression but from present responsibility. Rebellion against all authority and determination to get out of the revolution what each individual or group wanted for itself led to an increasingly anarchic situation. Finally, the growing frustration and resentment the masses felt when the revolution did not at once fulfill their needs and desires drove them to stronger and more forceful demands.

At the same time that these factors were working their radical spell, physical conditions of life in Russia were deteriorating at a breakneck pace. Despair over what had not happened and anger over what was happening made an explosive combination. For the city dweller, the problems of daily existence that had led directly to the outburst against the tsarist regime a few months previously worsened in the summer of 1917. Shortages of essentials and soaring inflation soon made survival dependent on ingenuity, luck, and contacts. The bread ration in Petrograd fell from one pound a day per inhabitant to one-half pound, while food prices in general are estimated to have doubled. Real wages declined by one-quarter to one-third, and unemployment increased dramatically as factories closed because of shortages of essential supplies or because of strikes and lockouts. Violence and lawlessness spread in the cities as N. N. Sukhanov, a Menshevik chronicler of the revolution, recalls:

> Lynchings, breaking into homes and shops, acts of violence against officers, provincial authorities, private persons, arbitrary arrest, seizures, and acts of vengeance—were registered daily in dozens and hundreds. . . . Soldiers, without any permission, poured homeward in enormous floods. They filled up all the railroads, attacking the officials, throwing out passengers. . . . And in the cities they overcrowded and destroyed the

streetcars and boulevards, filled up all public places. There also one heard of drunkenness and disorder.[3]

In the countryside labor was still in short supply despite the return to the farms of some soldier-deserters anxious to share in the rumored distribution of land. Prices still squeezed the peasant unfavorably, and the continuing collapse of the transport system made it difficult either to move grain to the cities, should the peasant decide to part with it, or to bring manufactured goods to the villages on the rare occasions when they were available. The peasant economy became increasingly cut off, which only worsened the supply crisis in the cities. As the minister of food explained, "We cannot take grain by force, the peasants don't want to take money, they must be supplied with those city products which they need. But there isn't enough of these products; there is no iron, no leather."[4]

The situation in non-Russian areas was exacerbated by the rapid spread of nationalist sentiment. The two most serious threats to centralized control by the Provisional government came from Finland and the Ukraine, although movements for autonomy also began to gain ground in the Caucasus and in Latvia. Left-wing nationalists in Finland demanded the withdrawal of all Russian troops and proposed that Finnish autonomy, approved earlier by the Provisional government, be extended to include all matters except foreign affairs.

Growing separatist feelings in the Ukraine posed an even more urgent danger for the Provisional government. The Ukraine was not only directly behind the battle lines at the southern end of the Eastern Front but was a major grain-producing area and contained rich coal and iron mines and prosperous industries. Begun in the nineteenth century by intellectuals, the Ukrainian nationalist movement had long focused on restoration of Ukrainian language and literature and development of an autonomous Ukrainian

[3] Quoted in William Henry Chamberlin, *The Russian Revolution, 1917–1921* (2 vols., New York, 1935; reprinted 1965), I, p. 153.
[4] *Ibid.*, p. 155.

culture. After the February Revolution, however, an all-Ukrainian representative council, called the Rada, was formed. In the libertarian and disintegrative atmosphere that followed the collapse of the old order, the Rada began to press for political autonomy for the Ukraine. As noted earlier, the Provisional government was reluctant to grant this, practically because it weakened the war effort and in principle because the government believed that only the Constituent Assembly could decide such a fundamental issue. By the end of June the Rada was acting, in defiance of the Petrograd authorities, as the virtual government of the Ukraine, although it stopped short of complete separation from the Russian state.

In this same period, the plight of the workers worsened and they came into frequent conflict with factory owners and the government. In retrospect, two factors seem responsible for the breakdown in labor relations that often led to lockouts or to workers seizing the factories. One was the actual conditions and problems both labor and management faced; the other was the atmosphere of mutual suspicion and recrimination in which the two groups wrestled with their difficulties.

From management's point of view, keeping businesses running became almost impossible. Sporadic and often unpredictable shortages of fuel and raw materials, compounded by transportation delays and breakdowns, meant the frequent interruption of production. Government interference through higher taxes, proliferating regulations, and various commissions and boards was, factory owners argued, disruptive and demanding. Finally, the workers, emboldened by the spirit of revolution, socialist propaganda, and the appalling conditions of urban life, increasingly violated labor discipline and continually escalated their demands until management claimed it was impossible to keep production going and the factory had to be closed.

On the workers' side, their wages did not rise nearly as rapidly as prices did. Although the government and the Soviet had agreed in principle on an eight-hour workday, not all factory owners observed it. Moreover, despite promises made at the time of the revolution, working conditions in the factories were not much changed and workers were still subject to oppression by abusive foremen and tyrannical bosses. Finally, unemployment increased in most of the industrial centers as the economic crisis deepened and production declined.

Both sides had real problems and legitimate grievances, and their difficulties were compounded by each group's distrust of the other. Many managers considered the workers uneducated, uncouth rabble who should be treated not with respect and concern but with firm discipline and considerable contempt. The workers' demands seemed unreasonable and covetous. The factory owners also feared the socialist drift of the working-class movement and deplored the growing disrespect for property rights. The workers appeared to be using the revolution as an excuse for getting something for nothing. The workers, on the other hand, became convinced that the industrialists were glutting themselves with exorbitant war profits and using the unsettled conditions to squeeze and exploit the workers even more. They felt that production stoppages and lockouts were weapons being used to drive wages down and weaken the working-class movement.

As the economic situation deteriorated, abuse and mistrust between the two groups increased. Given the owners' willingness to close the plants, the workers found strikes less and less helpful in defending their position. Before long they began—often spontaneously, sometimes stimulated by Bolshevik propaganda—to demand a voice in the running of the factories and then to occupy them if their demand was not met. By mid-June workers' committees dominated by Bolsheviks were intervening more and more in the management of industries in Petrograd; a month or so later workers had actually seized and were operating numerous factories throughout the country in a movement known as "workers' control."

As often happened, the government was unable to act decisively. It did not have the force to stem this anarchic tide but even if it had had, it lacked the will. Several of the socialist ministers in the coalition cabinet were well aware of the desperate conditions in which the workers worked and lived and wanted to side with them.

Yet they were also committed to keeping the war effort going and so could do little but halfheartedly urge the workers to stop their seizures of factories.

The revolutionary expropriation of factories remained on a fairly small scale during the summer of 1917. But the seizure of land by the peasants that began in the same period was wide-ranging and momentous. It amounted to a major social revolution which the Bolsheviks, after they came to power, had to accept despite its violation of Marxist ideology and which they were able to reverse, some twelve years later during the collectivization of agriculture, only at the cost of millions of lives. The powerful engine of this vast upheaval was land hunger. We discussed some of the reasons for the peasants' desperate need for more land in Chapter One. Now, in the wake of the revolution, they took it. If the owners resisted, the peasants often resorted to force, stealing tools and seed, destroying movable property, burning manor houses, and occasionally killing those who stood in their way. Peasants in the villages were often joined by peasant deserters from the army who had brought their rifles home with them.

This peasant revolution gathered momentum throughout the summer of 1917. One estimate shows 174 peasant disorders reported in April, 325 in July, and 686 between July and October.[5] There was little the government or anyone else could do. The authorities patiently explained to the peasants that such a basic issue as land reform could not be decided unilaterally by the government or by the peasants but must await resolution in the Constituent Assembly, which would represent the wishes of all the Russian people. The peasants listened politely, waited a little while, then began taking the land. The government set up a national commission and agricultural committees in the districts to begin preparations for land reform. But since these committees could only collect information, take over uncultivated land, and urge patience, the peasants soon began to ignore them. Moreover, many peasants lost faith in the promises of the officials; for exam-

[5] Marcel Liebman, *The Russian Revolution,* trans. Arnold J. Pomerans (New York, 1972), p. 141.

Rural raw material for revolution: Russian peasants in the main street of a typical village. *Keystone Press Agency Inc.*

ple, the government said it would not permit private landowners to sell their holdings to outsiders, yet many landowners were able to circumvent the regulations and do just that, and the peasants were fully aware of this.

At last, in an effort to check the increase in land seizures, the government lectured and threatened the peasants, as in this appeal by Chernov, the minister of agriculture: "The settlement of agricultural disputes by local action cannot be tolerated . . . such arbitrary acts are bound to lead to national disaster."[6] Such warnings did little good. The peasants believed that by ancient tradition the land was theirs to use, and the government simply did not have the power to enforce its temporizing policies. Thus the movement swept on, involving millions of people and millions of acres of land. The Bolsheviks had little to do with this anarchic revolution but supported it in their program, thereby winning over some peasants and neutralizing others.

Although the radical actions of national minorities, workers, and peasants all eroded the position of the Provisional government, the

[6] *Ibid.*, p. 144.

decisive factor that undercut its ability to survive was the disintegration of the army. In the Revolution of 1905, when things looked blackest the tsarist government was able to send reliable troops into the fray. By the fall of 1917 the Provisional government did not have dependable military forces at its disposal; indeed, no group committed to continuing the war could have had.

What changed the mind of the revolutionary but patriotic soldier of the February Revolution? At that time he had been determined to reject the old order but seemed willing to defend the country against the Germans. What made him, in a matter of weeks, into a mutinous barracks-room lounger or a deserter? It is not enough to maintain that the average Russian soldier didn't want to be killed in a war he didn't understand; he had been willing to face an inexplicable death a few months previously. To blame Order No. 1 or Bolshevik propaganda, as some writers have done, is also inadequate; the disintegration of the army did not occur until some time after Order No. 1 had been issued, and the Bolsheviks never had enough resources to blanket the army with agitators and materials. Some critics have maintained that the attitude of the Petrograd Soviet leadership was responsible for the erosion of military morale because they exhorted the soldiers to fight in a war they themselves criticized and obviously did not believe in; yet many soldiers who were unaware of this subtle contradiction still became mutinous.

As in most cases of historical explanation, the sudden collapse of the Russian army undoubtedly had a number of causes, including those mentioned above. In my view, however, an overriding reason for this phenomenon can be found in the psychology of the average soldier. Under the tsarist regime he obeyed and sacrificed out of duty, out of loyalty to the tsar, out of fear of punishment, out of inertia. How long the tsarist army could have held together on this basis is indeed questionable; signs of strain and dissolution were growing before the February Revolution. But once the revolution occurred and the libertarian spirit we have referred to before permeated the population, the old ties, the old reasons for following orders and being killed, disappeared. The soldier, at first in the garrisons and rear lines but before long in the trenches, repudiated the traditional system, embodied for him by the tsar and his officers. He simply would no longer respond to goals and slogans which held little direct meaning to him. No new norms (except the fuzzy revolutionary grandiloquence of Kerensky) existed to guide the average soldier. Neither more just and more meaningful war aims nor the democratization of the army could satisfy the Russian soldier for long, although undoubtedly he wanted these changes. Now he was freed of all previous restraints and obligations, and there was little the Soviet or the Provisional government could say or do that would lead him to follow the beat of a new drummer. Increasingly the Russian soldier saw that he could take things into his own hands and shape his own destiny. He wanted to stop the bloodshed and to go home to his village, land, and family. He felt he no longer had to serve the interests of the masters under whose yoke he had bent for over three hundred years. Seeing no need to fight or to obey, he refused to do anything, or he mutinied and deserted. Formal military force was no longer a factor in the revolution from the late summer of 1917 on—though few realized it at the time.

THE GATHERING STORM

Before the launching of the July Offensive and while the first All-Russian Congress of Soviets was still meeting, an episode occurred that dramatically reflected the radicalization of the urban masses and clearly signaled the shape of the future. The pivotal event was a popular demonstration planned for June 23 in Petrograd.

Bolsheviks played an important role in this episode, but their actions can be understood only in light of the special position and complex character of the party in Petrograd, as the American historian Alexander Rabinowitch has traced it.[7] Since the February Revolution, tens of thousands of recruits had joined the Bolshevik party. In the capital these new members came largely from the more

[7] Alexander Rabinowitch, *Prelude to Revolution: The Petrograd Bolsheviks and the July 1917 Uprising* (Bloomington, Ind., 1968).

radical workers and from some of the garrison units. Their understanding of Marxism was limited but their basic attitudes and demands were extremely revolutionary. This swelling of the party's ranks at the lowest levels exerted pressure for more radical policies upward through district committees. The Bolshevik leadership at the top, however, was neither closely coordinated nor always in agreement, much less a monolithic unity as some writers have portrayed it.

In Petrograd the three most important bodies of the party were the Central Committee, which was the top executive of the whole party, the Petersburg (City) Committee, and the Military Organization. The Central Committee, which had to keep in mind the situation throughout the country and particularly the possibility that the peasantry might not support an immediate seizure of power by the Bolsheviks, was naturally more cautious in its attitudes and actions. Lenin himself, while espousing the slogan "All Power to the Soviets," was keenly aware that the soviets were still in the hands of the Mensheviks and SRs, who would oppose a Bolshevik move to seize power. He also recognized that a Bolshevik revolution, even if successful in Petrograd, might provoke counter-revolution outside the capital.

Both Lenin and the Central Committee of the party frequently had to contend with the more radical views and policies of the Petersburg Committee and the Military Organization. The former, which had retained its name as a token of its opposition to the war even after St. Petersburg had been renamed Petrograd, reflected the views of lower party units that were in daily touch with the workers. It thus espoused a revolutionary line sooner and more readily than Lenin and the Central Committee and demanded steps that more closely accorded with the aspirations of the masses. Set up in March to agitate and organize in the Petrograd garrison and at the Kronstadt naval base, the Military Organization was soon given responsibility for revolutionizing all the armed forces. Though the mass of soldiers was fairly conservative, the Military Organization frequently built on the most radical elements in army and navy units, and its own leaders took a particularly aggressive and revolutionary line.

By the middle of June the masses in Petrograd were obviously restless, and their radical feelings seemed to be running far in advance not only of the position of the moderate socialist leadership of the Soviet but even ahead of the stance of the Bolshevik party. There was a looming danger that the Bolsheviks would lose the support of the more radical elements if the party did not move to keep up with them. The leadership therefore approved, rather reluctantly, the idea of a mass demonstration in Petrograd, a proposal urged on them by local party units and supported independently by other revolutionary elements in the capital, including the anarchists. Plans for the demonstration were kept secret so that the Mensheviks and SRs could neither interfere nor arrange a counterdemonstration.

The Bolshevik leaders wanted the demonstration to be large but peaceful; suggestions for occupying public buildings and other revolutionary acts were turned down. The chief slogan was to be "All Power to the Soviets." As the day of the demonstration approached, however, it became clear that the Bolsheviks were going to have difficulty keeping the demonstration within bounds. Several military units decided to take part but without promising to leave their weapons behind, and hotheaded leaders kept pressing for more forceful action. An armed clash with the government, resulting in bloodshed and probably unfavorable political repercussions, seemed more and more likely.

At this point the leaders of the Petrograd Soviet got wind of the plans and the Soviet executive committee banned the demonstration. The Bolsheviks considered ignoring the ban, but it was endorsed shortly by the All-Russian Congress of Soviets, then in session, which resolved that anyone defying the Soviet's prohibition would be considered "an enemy of the Revolution." Lenin wavered, but finally went along with a decision late on the evening of June 22 to call off the demonstration. This was easier said than done, however. It took the most strenuous exhortations of Bolshevik and Soviet agitators sent to the factories and barracks to persuade the workers and soldiers not to come out on the streets next day.

In an attempt to appease the angry and disappointed masses, to show up the Bolsheviks, and to win popular support for themselves, the moderate socialists in the Soviet decided to organize their own demonstration. It was held on July 1, but it served only the first of its intended aims; otherwise it strengthened the Bolsheviks and weakened the moderate socialists. The crowds were enormous—estimated at 400,000 people—but orderly. It was a tense and exciting spectacle to see the massed ranks parading down Petrograd's main street, Nevsky Prospect, with huge banners bearing boldly daubed slogans. Occasionally contrasted with these were the black banners of the anarchists. The slogans were the key to the sentiment of the throngs. The Soviet leaders had declared as official slogans for the demonstration "Universal Peace," "Immediate Convocation of a Constituent Assembly," and "A Democratic Republic." A few banners bore these words but were far outnumbered and overshadowed by the sea of Bolshevik slogans being carried along: "DOWN WITH THE TEN CAPITALIST MINISTERS," "DOWN WITH THE OFFENSIVE," and "ALL POWER TO THE SOVIETS." The moderate socialists' demonstration had turned into a triumphal procession in support of the Bolsheviks.

This episode in the history of the revolution ended without further notable events. Yet it contained several significant portents. The urban lower classes in Petrograd proved to be far more susceptible to the ideas of the Bolsheviks and the anarchists than anyone had suspected. Their feelings were far outrunning the views of the moderate socialist leaders of the Soviet. The crowds were also becoming increasingly hard to control. Popular resentment against the Provisional government, indeed against all authority, was growing rapidly.

For the government the signs were ominous, though the June events did not lead to any change in its basic policies, partly because of the high hopes for redressing the situation that both Soviet and governmental leaders placed in the imminent military offensive. The government simply had no influence with the masses, who responded, if at all, only to the pleas of Soviet and Bolshevik leaders.

For the Bolsheviks this series of events created some perplexing dilemmas. How far could they restrain the radical crowds without losing their support? Could they both lead and control the masses? If a revolutionary uprising occurred, would this not provoke a reaction which would halt the revolution and end the Bolsheviks' chances of eventually coming to power? In the next few weeks new developments forced the party to confront these questions in a virtually "no-win" situation, as we shall see shortly.

The June events marked an important turning point in the history of the revolution. In retrospect we can see that the radicalization of the urban masses in Petrograd had gone so far that only a fundamental alteration of policy by the Soviet leaders and the Provisional government would have had any chance of checking or reversing that leftward movement. As in the days before the February Revolution, the gap between the rulers and the ruled was rapidly becoming unbridgeable and understanding between the two seemed impossible. The revolution was clearly approaching a crisis. The unstable equilibrium between popular sentiment that was increasingly pacifist, radical, and liberationist and a government committed to legality and the war could not last. Something was bound to happen—and it soon did.

5
Summer Crises

★

During the summer of 1917 Russia experienced two major crises, either of which might have turned the course of revolution in an entirely new direction. In both cases the Provisional government was seriously endangered but survived. The first threat was a mass protest against the government and the existing situation by radical workers and soldiers in Petrograd; the events associated with this protest are known as the July Days. The second was an attempt by the army commander, General Lavr G. Kornilov, supported by conservative groups, to suppress leftist elements in the capital (by force if necessary), to reestablish discipline in the army, and perhaps to set up a counterrevolutionary government; it is known as the Kornilov affair. Neither effort succeeded, and in the long run the Bolsheviks benefited greatly from both crises. The inability of the crowds to seize power on their own and the failure of counterrevolution from the right opened the door to a directed mass uprising under Bolshevik leadership once it became clear that the Provisional government was powerless either to complete or to halt the revolution.

POPULAR INSURRECTION: THE JULY DAYS

It was July 17, less than three weeks after the massive peaceful demonstration called by the Petrograd Soviet that had turned into a triumphal march in support of the Bolsheviks. But now the crowds in Petrograd were disorderly and angry. Throngs of demonstrators, hangers-on, and the curious were moving along Nevsky Prospect, the main street of Petrograd, when several rifle shots popped sharply, quickly followed by a staccato burst of shooting from various directions as those in the throng who had weapons responded in panic, aimlessly. The crowd scattered, running, but a number fell to the pavement—some dead, more wounded.

Down the street a small group of sailors from Kronstadt who had come to join the demonstration that morning ran into a building from which they thought rifle fire had come. In the hallway a few shots reverberated as the Kronstadters wreaked vengeance on whatever person, guilty or innocent, they found inside. Along several side streets looters smashed shop windows and broke open cupboards and cases to take what was available. On Liteiny Prospect rioters tore down streetcar cables, and elsewhere in the city transportation was blocked by the crowds roaming the streets.

Near the center of town the leaders of the Soviet were meeting in the Tauride Palace. Outside, demonstrators massed, dispersed, and regrouped. Those inside the building were quite defenseless, but the crowds in the street did not know precisely what to do; their confusion symbolized the July Days.

No particular event touched off the riots of July 16 and 17. Some textbooks explain it as a response to the failure of the July military offensive, but in fact the news that the offensive had collapsed did not reach Petrograd until July 18. The explosion resulted fundamentally from the deteriorating conditions of daily life, from mounting frustration over the government's failure to fulfill popular aspirations, and from elemental distrust and deep-seated hatred of the upper classes. In addition, workers had specific economic grievances and garrison soldiers were anxious to avoid being sent to the front.

Relations between labor and management grew steadily worse in the summer of 1917. Some plants were forced to close because of a lack of fuel or raw materials. Sporadic strikes and lockouts were followed by attempts by workers to intervene in the running of factories or to seize them. Part of the discontent that sparked the July Days stemmed from unrest at the Putilov works, which inflamed other disputes and created tension and anxiety in the working-class districts of the city.

At the same time, the garrison soldiers were becoming increasingly restive. In May, shortly after becoming minister of war, Kerensky had issued a Declaration of Soldiers' Rights which, while incorporating many of the soldiers' demands, fell short of meeting them all. During June and early July the troops in barracks, stirred up by their own and Bolshevik agitators, became increasingly aggrieved over the shortcomings of the declaration. Then, in early July, when the offensive was being readied, furloughs granted to soldiers over forty years of age to return to the farms to help with the summer's crops were suddenly canceled. Finally, just before the offensive, units of the Petrograd garrison began to be ordered to the front. In the First Machine Gun Regiment, which for some time had been under radical influence, the soldiers' committees decided that only ten detachments of the thirty ordered up would go.

At this moment the coalition cabinet of the Provisional government fell apart, and the country was without even nominal authority. The cabinet formed in May contained four ministers from the Kadet party. As lawlessness in the country increased and the populace in Petrograd became more unruly, the Kadets began to doubt the logic that had led them into the coalition. They had hoped that accepting socialist ministers in the cabinet would calm the masses, restore order, and facilitate launching the offensive. With the last about to be accomplished, it was glaringly evident that neither of the first two purposes had been achieved. Moreover, the socialists seemed to be escalating their demands within the government. They were pressing for economic concessions to the workers, a more liberal land policy, and a more conciliatory attitude toward the national minorities. All this was finally too much

for the Kadets and their leader, Miliukov, who remained somewhat embittered over his ouster from the cabinet two months
previously. When the government's socialist leadership, without
consulting the full cabinet, negotiated an agreement with the
Ukrainian Rada which seemed to the Kadets to give the Ukrainians
too much autonomy, the Kadet ministers resigned on July 15,
precipitating a governmental crisis.

The tense atmosphere in the city and the upheaval in the government over the Ukrainian issue placed the Bolsheviks in an extremely uncomfortable position. Their local and district leaders
were warning that the masses' volatile feelings could not be contained much longer. To let the radical workers and soldiers act
alone would mean losing influence over them. To encourage them
would almost certainly lead to a premature uprising and counterrevolutionary suppression. The dilemma first posed at the time of
the June demonstration now reemerged acutely and urgently.
Moreover, as noted earlier, the Bolshevik leadership was far from
united on what strategy should be pursued.

The Military Organization included several firebrands who were
urging that the opportune moment for armed insurrection had arrived. More cautious leaders in the Central Committee of the party
believed that the bourgeois-democratic phase of the revolution
had not been completed and that an organized effort to topple the
government would be adventuristic and dangerous. Lenin, usually
the most certain and forceful leader, was unsure what to do.[1] Lenin
was still clinging to his slogan "All Power to the Soviets" but he was
aware that the Menshevik and Socialist Revolutionary leaders of the
Soviet did not want sole power even if the masses thrust it upon
them. Lenin believed that a Bolshevik attempt to seize power
would be premature, yet he feared that not to lead the masses
would weaken the Bolsheviks' hold on them. Thus with their top
leaders hesitant and uncertain, the Bolsheviks were in considerable
disarray when the masses took to the streets.

The storm broke on the morning of July 16. The initiative came
from the First Machine Gun Regiment. Radicals in the regiment

[1] Alexander Rabinowitch, *Prelude to Revolution: The Petrograd Bolsheviks
and the July 1917 Uprising* (Bloomington, Ind., 1968), chs. V and VI.

decided to demonstrate with arms, both against the sending of units to the front and for the overthrow of the Provisional government. Although the Bolshevik Central Committee tried to head off the demonstration, arguing that it was not adequately prepared or organized, by evening envoys from the machine gunners had persuaded two other regiments to join them. Squads of armed soldiers soon began arriving at Bolshevik headquarters. The Bolshevik leaders in Petrograd (Lenin was away; he returned the following morning) had already decided to issue an appeal in *Pravda* (Truth), the party newspaper, the next day calling the planned demonstration inopportune. Now under the direct pressure of the masses in the streets the Central Committee reversed this decision and determined to try to assume direction of the mass movement and to organize a peaceful demonstration on July 17. It was too late to replace the article in *Pravda* so it was simply deleted, the newspaper appearing next morning with a glaring blank space on the front page.

The leaders of the Soviet were irate but powerless. They pleaded with the soldiers to return to their barracks, reminding them that they were not to act without authorization of the government and the Soviet. But the demonstrators were in no mood to listen. They continued to mill about until late at night on the 16th, demanding that the Soviet leaders assume power. The latter adamantly refused, the All-Russian Executive Committee passing late on July 16 a sternly worded resolution:

> Some armed military units have come out on the streets, attempting to master the city, seizing automobiles, arresting at their will individuals, operating with threats and violence. Coming . . . with arms in their hands, they demanded that the Executive Committees assume all power. Proposing power to the Soviets they are the first to attack this power. The All-Russian executive organs . . . reject with indignation every attempt to bring pressure on their free will. It is unworthy to attempt by means of armed demonstrations to impose the will of some parts of the garrison of one city upon all Russia.[2]

[2] Quoted in William Henry Chamberlin, *The Russian Revolution, 1917–1921* (2 vols., New York, 1935; reprinted 1965), I, p. 171.

Eyewitness accounts make clear that the mood of the crowds in the July Days was far different from the congenial, enthusiastic spirit that had animated the throngs during the February Revolution and even in some of the spring demonstrations. The July crowds were angry and unruly; they did not hesitate to resort to violence. While clearer understanding of this shift of attitude must await detailed study of the psychology of the Russian revolutionary masses like the analyses made of the crowds in the French Revolution, it is possible to speculate concerning the demonstrators' sentiments in the July Days. One important factor in the protestors' mood was undoubtedly a feeling of deprivation. Their psychological sense of loss was enormous. Everyone, but particularly the lower classes, had expected great things from the revolution: it was somehow to solve all their problems. Now, four months later, none of these great expectations had been fulfilled. And people were beginning to realize that there was little likelihood that they would be soon. Disappointment was turning rapidly to anger, which in the new freedom brought by the revolution could be expressed by lashing out at whatever and whomever seemed responsible for the dashing of their hopes.

Another aspect of the popular mood was intense frustration. In July the masses were not lethargic as they had become by the time of the October Revolution. They wanted to do something, to act, in order to better their lot and to achieve what they expected from the revolution. But they didn't know what to do, how to act. They felt vaguely that if only the Soviet, which after all was supposed to represent them and act for them, would take power, everything would be all right. But the Soviet leaders kept saying, in terms the average worker and soldier could hardly be expected to understand, that they could not take power. This was surely maddening and embittering to the crowds.

Finally, the behavior of the crowds in July almost certainly reflected the growing anarchic element in the revolution that we have noted previously. From the joys of liberation to the denial of all authority, the throwing off of all restraints, was a fairly short step in the Russian society of 1917.

On July 17 the demonstrators were out in force again, more disorderly than on the previous day despite Bolshevik efforts to assume direction of the movement. The situation was inflamed by the arrival by boat of some 20,000 radical sailors from Kronstadt. Both the Soviet and the government were helpless. Those units which had not joined the machine gunners remained in their barracks, declaring themselves "neutral." More reliable elements that had been ordered to the capital from outside would not arrive until evening. The demonstrators could have done anything they pleased; but they did not know what to do. Their avowed aim was to transfer power to the Soviet; when its leaders refused this gift, the crowds were left purposeless and turned increasingly to panicky violence. Some four or five hundred people were killed and wounded in the July Days, mainly on July 17.

With no clear goal left, the demonstration began to peter out by the night of July 17. The end of the disorders was hastened when the minister of justice of the outgoing cabinet, encouraged by Kerensky, released documents alleging that Lenin was a German agent and that the Bolsheviks were in the pay of Germany. These rumors swept swiftly through the capital; two regiments that had remained neutral now decided to come to the support of the Soviet and the government. By midday on July 18 loyal troops were patroling the streets, which were now almost free of angry demonstrators. On the 19th, the last of the Kronstadt sailors were persuaded to return to their island base, and what Lenin called "something considerably more than a demonstration but less than a revolution" was over.

In the reaction against the Bolsheviks that immediately began, the charge that they were German agents weighed heavily. The information on which the allegation was based was so skimpy and the evidence of such doubtful credibility that several ministers opposed making it public, while the prime minister, Prince Lvov, asked to no avail that newspapers not publish the documents until an investigative commission could look into the matter. German records that have come to light since World War II show that German intelligence authorities did supply money to the Bolshe-

The "July Days" in Petrograd: Street crowds on Nevsky Prospekt, the city's main thoroughfare, scatter during a random shooting as casualties fall to the pavement. *United Press International Photo*

viks through Sweden. Lenin was undoubtedly aware of this but was perfectly willing to accept funds from any source, including Russia's wartime foes. Although it makes the indignant Bolshevik denials of the time sound a bit disingenuous, the fact that Lenin took German money did not make him a German agent any more than his earlier acceptance of German assistance in returning to Russia did. Lenin and the Bolsheviks were not out to assist Germany but to further their own ends; in fact, they expected that revolution in Russia would be the spark needed to overthrow the German government and touch off socialist revolution in the rest of Europe. For their part, the Germans wanted to foment revolution in Russia in order to disrupt an enemy war effort and were happy to aid anyone whom they thought might be useful in that regard—and indeed they provided funds to other Russian radicals and separatists as well as to revolutionaries in Ireland who were making trouble for the English.

At the time, however, the ill-supported accusations against the Bolsheviks helped swing large segments of public opinion behind the government. War-weariness was growing and patriotism declining, but at a time when thousands of Russians were dying in the abortive offensive, many found it galling to hear that German spies and traitors in the sheep's clothing of radicals were at large in the capital itself. Kerensky ordered the Bolshevik newspaper, *Pravda,* raided and then closed, and the main offices of the party were seized. Within a few days the government arrested several prominent Bolsheviks, including Kamenev and Trotsky, together with several hundred rank-and-file party members.

Within top party circles a brief debate ensued about what course Lenin should follow. If he let himself be arrested, what were his chances of receiving a fair trial and what were the risks of a trigger-happy guard shooting him? If he went into hiding, would it not be considered an admission of guilt, thereby further weakening the party's position? Both sides of the question were persuasively argued, but Lenin himself finally became convinced that any trial would be a travesty of justice and would leave the party without its chief leader at a crucial time. He therefore shaved off his beard and slipped out of Petrograd dressed as a workman, hiding first in a small town twenty miles from the capital and later in a rustic cabin in Finland, which was still part of Russia. There he wrote his famous tract *State and Revolution* while remaining in fairly close touch with party affairs through messages and couriers. He did not return to Petrograd until a short time before the October Revolution.

News from the front of the failure of the offensive intensified the reaction against the Bolsheviks. In the face of this disheartening defeat, moderates and conservatives appealed urgently for all elements in Russian society to unite and work for restoration of order and legality. On July 21 Kerensky replaced Prince Lvov as prime minister. Although it took him more than two weeks to patch together a new coalition cabinet of socialists and nonsocialists, in the interim he ordered several of the mutinous regiments broken up, closed Bolshevik printing presses, banned Bolshevik newspapers from all theaters of military operations, and had factories searched for illegal arms possessed by workers. The government also restored the death penalty at the front and attempted to enforce discipline in the army more vigorously. It held a solemn state funeral for seven Cossacks killed by rioters during the July Days, at which Kerensky orated:

> Before all of you I openly declare that all attempts to foment anarchy and disorder regardless of where they come from will be dealt with mercilessly. . . . Before the bodies of the fallen, I beseech you to swear that along with us you will work to save the state and freedom.[3]

Raising his right hand, Kerensky declared, "I pledge this!" In response the crowd shouted back, "We swear it!"[4] In this sort of atmosphere it is not surprising that workers suspected of being Bolsheviks were beaten up and that Lenin believed it unlikely

---

[3] Quoted in Alexander Rabinowitch, *The Bolsheviks Come to Power: The Revolution of 1917 in Petrograd* (New York, 1976), p. 41.
[4] *Ibid.*

August 1917—V. I. Lenin in hiding in Finland working on revolutionary plans. *The Copyright Agency of the USSR*

that he could obtain a fair trial. Even socialists who were not Bolsheviks were harassed and occasionally arrested.

The July Days had repercussions outside of Petrograd as well. Demonstrations in support of those in the capital occurred in a number of cities, but in only a few industrial centers did these have even fleeting success. In Moscow the Bolsheviks organized a peaceful demonstration, but most workers did not participate, responding to a prohibition by the Moscow Soviet against meetings and demonstrations. There were more effective demonstrations in several towns in the central-industrial region of Russia and in several provincial capitals. In Nizhni-Novgorod a revolutionary committee temporarily seized power, but representatives of the Moscow Soviet soon arrived to restore order and to arrest the ringleaders of the uprising.

By the last days of July the Provisional government appeared much strengthened and the Bolsheviks greatly weakened. But appearances were deceiving. The government had become, for almost everyone, a necessary evil, tolerated by many but not enthusiastically supported in any quarter. Military authorities and conservatives blamed it for the decline of the fighting capacity of the army and for disorder and lack of discipline on the home front. They would have been happy to replace it but at the moment saw no feasible alternative. Thus, to keep the war effort going, they had to put up with it. Industrialists and landowners distrusted the socialist cast of the government and decried the continuing seizures of land and factories, but they recognized that an all-capitalist government might provoke a full popular revolution and that an all-socialist government might move to legalize the distribution of land and the takeover of factories. The moderate socialist leaders, having rejected the power the masses wanted to give them on July 16 and 17, had no choice but to continue in partnership with nonsocialists. They hoped to preserve the freedoms of the revolution, prevent capitalist reaction, and move the country toward social reform. But they remained committed to the war and clung to the principle that final decisions about dividing the land must await convocation of the Constituent Assembly. The workers and soldiers disliked and distrusted the government but having had their offer of power to the Soviet rejected, they too had no alternative for the moment.

Meanwhile, the demand for peace continued to grow, the workers were as insistent as ever on improvement of their economic situation and living conditions, the peasants went on occupying and dividing the land, and anti-Russian sentiment continued to spread among the national minorities. The government made no important changes in its basic positions and policies; hence there was no possibility that it could enhance its authority or prestige.

With these factors in mind, one is tempted to wonder whether the Bolsheviks might not have carried the day if they had acted earlier and more decisively during the July upheavals. Once it had become clear that an explosion was imminent, the Bolsheviks might have done the necessary planning, made the required preparations, and carefully organized a full-scale armed insurrection. In retrospect it is clear that they could have seized the capital on July 16 and 17. What is not certain is whether they could have retained power.

In my view, several factors suggest that they could not have. First, the disintegration of the army had not yet proceeded far enough to neutralize the role of armed force in the country as a whole. Reliable units and officers willing to defend the government could undoubtedly have been summoned from the front and other parts of Russia to quell any Bolshevik insurrection in Petrograd. Four months later, the officers despised the government and there were virtually no reliable units. Second, although tens of thousands rioted and the masses clearly favored Bolshevik slogans, the July demonstrators were not asking that the Bolsheviks take over but that the Soviet should; their faith was not in a party but in the elected body that represented them. Moreover, in July other tens of thousands of workers and soldiers were still under Menshevik and SR influence and would probably have opposed a Bolshevik coup d'état if the moderate socialist leaders had asked them to. Finally, and most important, a vital element was missing in the atmosphere of July—the fear of counterrevolution. At that moment the Bolsheviks could hardly argue that they were saving the revolution from its enemies; but once counterrevolution had actually been attempted, this became a powerful argument for winning over moderates and apolitical elements in the country.

ABORTIVE COUNTERREVOLUTION: THE KORNILOV AFFAIR

During World War I an important method of communication was a direct telegraphic device, somewhat like a modern telex, through which two parties could transmit directly to each other. In 1917 such an instrument linked the Russian ministry of war in Petrograd and the Stavka, headquarters of the army general staff in the town of Mogilev. On the evening of September 8 this line of communication was used for a fateful conversation between Prime Minister Kerensky and General Kornilov, whom Kerensky had appointed commander-in-chief of the army six weeks previously. Part of the conversation went like this:

KERENSKY: Good day, General. . . . We beg you to confirm the statement that Kerensky is to act according to the communication made to him by Vladimir Nikolaevich [Lvov, a self-appointed intermediary between Kornilov and Kerensky].

KORNILOV: Good day. . . . I declare again that the events of the past days and of those that I can see coming imperatively demand a definite decision in the shortest possible time.

[Later in the conversation] Yes, I confirm . . . my urgent plea that he [Kerensky] should come to Mogilev. . . .

KERENSKY: Shall we come only in case of an outbreak, of which there are rumors, or in any case?

KORNILOV: In any case.

KERENSKY: Good-by. We shall soon see each other.

KORNILOV: Good-by.[5]

For Kerensky the conversation confirmed his worst fears that Kornilov was preparing to overthrow the Provisional government, replace Kerensky, and establish himself as military dictator. Kerensky's intimation that he would go to Mogilev—which he had no intention of doing—led Kornilov to think that Kerensky had agreed to cooperate in Kornilov's plans for restoring discipline in the army, suppressing radicalism in the capital, and setting up a strong government. A tragicomedy of unrealistic plotting and mutual misunderstandings begun several weeks previously was nearly complete.

The Kornilov affair pursued a confused and tortuous course, mainly because the two principals, Kornilov and Kerensky, misled each other—and perhaps themselves. General Lavr G. Kornilov was a brave and forceful professional officer who first gained fame when in 1915 he escaped from the Austrians after being taken prisoner on the Galician Front. In the spring of 1917 he attracted the attention of conservatives when he requested transfer from his post as commander of the Petrograd Military District in disgust over the unruly behavior of the soldiers and workers and the government's unwillingness to use stern measures to restore discipline and order. Kornilov had considerable élan and magnetism. The son of a Siberian Cossack, he had a slightly Mongolian cast to his features and surrounded himself with a bodyguard of Turkmen soldiers, a fierce, devoted, and colorful entourage.

At the same time, Kornilov was quite ill-fitted to lead a counter-revolutionary movement. He knew little about politics or social issues. His views on the situation in Russia and what should be done were simplistic and limited. He was also a terribly vain and vaguely ambitious man. When people suggested that he should be the savior of Mother Russia, his head was easily turned and his

[5] Robert P. Browder and Alexander F. Kerensky (eds.), *The Russian Provisional Government 1917: Documents* (3 vols., Stanford, Calif., 1961), III, p. 1571.

judgment warped. Moreover, the combination of his susceptibility to flattery and his political naïveté caused him to be easily influenced by those around him and frequently to change his mind according to the last piece of advice he received. If his advisers had been abler men, this failing might not have been so serious, but they were second-rate politicians, intriguers, and bumblers.

Kerensky was also vain and changeable. He often reacted emotionally to situations and later thought better of what he had done and reversed himself. Although he was premier primarily because there was no one else on whom both socialists and nonsocialists could agree, he had some delusions of grandeur. Consequently, he reacted strongly when he finally appreciated that Kornilov threatened his position as head of the government and titular leader of the revolution. Up to that moment Kerensky had apparently thought he was using Kornilov for his own purposes—to strengthen the government and his position as premier—although Kerensky's motivations throughout the episode are not always entirely clear and his memoirs are too self-justificatory to be of much help in explaining his actions.

The crisis began at the end of July in the aftermath of the July Days and the disastrous offensive. After becoming prime minister, Kerensky had delegated much of the responsibility of running the ministry of war to Boris Savinkov, formerly a Socialist Revolutionary terrorist but now quite moderate in his views. Savinkov, previously the government's political representative on the Southwestern Front, which Kornilov commanded, had been impressed with Kornilov's performance during the ill-fated offensive and with his views on army reform. Partly because of Savinkov's recommendation and partly because at a conference of army commanders over which Kerensky presided Kornilov was the only general to submit a moderate and fairly optimistic report, Kerensky decided to make Kornilov commander-in-chief and to charge him with restoring the fighting capacity of the army. Kerensky undoubtedly hoped that Kornilov's reputation among conservatives and his record as a stern disciplinarian would win support for the government from the disgruntled generals and rightist politicians, while Kornilov's expressed willingness to work with army committees and commissars would make him acceptable to the Soviet leaders and moderates. Evidently it never crossed Kerensky's mind at that time that Kornilov might be a dangerous individual to have in supreme command of the army.

As a prerequisite of his accepting the supreme command Kornilov asked that the government accept several conditions. One was that the death penalty be restored among rear as well as front-line units. This was most unpopular with the soldiers and was opposed by the Soviet leaders, but Kerensky accepted it in principle. Kornilov also insisted that he intended to be responsible "before his own conscience and before the people." This suggested an independent political role for the supreme commander, but after some discussion Kornilov finally agreed that he would be responsible to the people through their representative, the Provisional government.

On August 16, a little over two weeks after becoming commander-in-chief, Kornilov visited Petrograd to press for broadened policy changes designed to rejuvenate the army. Two incidents during his stay in the capital were notable. In their first lengthy personal interview, Kerensky and Kornilov did not hit it off well at all. Kornilov evidently found Kerensky bombastic and elusive, while Kerensky saw Kornilov as ambitious and potentially dangerous. Later during his visit Kornilov was appalled when just before he entered a meeting of the full cabinet, including its socialist ministers, he was warned not to talk about any military secrets because the socialists frequently reported governmental business to the Soviet, whence it might reach the ears of German agents. From then on Kornilov apparently believed that the socialists and Soviet leaders were not only responsible for unrest and disorder in the rear but that they also were harboring spies, traitors, and saboteurs in their midst.

Kerensky, whose main concern for the past four months had been the reorganization and bolstering of the army, was genuinely anxious to support strict new measures toward that end and found little in Kornilov's program with which he disagreed. But news of what Kornilov was pressing for was leaked to the newspapers, stirring up a storm of criticism from leftist elements. Both Kerensky and his government were balanced precariously between right and left forces, and it was politically impossible for him to push Kornilov's program too vigorously or too quickly. Thus days dragged into weeks without firm government action on what Kornilov wanted done. To Kornilov, who had little understanding of the political situation, Kerensky appeared weak and devious. He apparently came to believe that Kerensky was reneging on his promises and that the government was too ineffectual to take the most elementary steps necessary to restore order and strengthen the army.

At this juncture Kornilov clearly became a rallying point for all those who were disgusted with disorder, lawlessness, the disintegration of the army, the vague socialism of the government, and Kerensky's spinelessness. The general was praised in the conservative press, castigated in the leftist papers. Rightist organizations issued laudatory pronouncements hailing him as the savior of Russia, while some in the Soviet demanded his replacement. Kornilov was apparently much flattered by the praise heaped on him from the right and began to see himself in a special role. On August 23 he passed word to Kerensky not to attempt to remove him as supreme commander.

Rumors of plots against the government flew about, and the radical press hinted darkly at Kadet participation. However, William Rosenberg has persuasively shown in his history of the Kadets during 1917 that this major liberal party was not involved in any conspiracy against Kerensky, though individual Kadets criticized the government and some undoubtedly were sympathetic to those right-wing and militaristic circles that were plotting to bring Kornilov to power.[6] The backroom scheming and disorganized maneuvering of the latter were, of course, totally inadequate to prepare the ground politically and publicly for a move against the government and the Soviet. They succeeded only in arousing fears

---

[6] William G. Rosenberg, *Liberals in the Russian Revolution: The Constitutional Democratic Party, 1917–1921* (Princeton, N.J., 1974).

of the army's interference in civil affairs and suspicion that all nonsocialists were dangerous counterrevolutionaries. Direct contacts and communication were eventually established between Kornilov's advisers at the Stavka and some extreme right-wing organizations in Petrograd, but the latter were too small and irresolute to be politically significant.

In the charged political atmosphere of the moment, it seemed evident that a showdown between Kerensky and Kornilov could not be long in coming. Great interest, therefore, centered on the Moscow State Conference, held from August 25 to 28. The government had planned the conference in the hope of promoting unity across the political spectrum and as a sounding board for its policies. During the reaction that followed the July Days some Duma deputies had called for reconvocation of the Duma until the Constituent Assembly could meet, but the Soviet leaders would never have agreed to this. Some in the government hoped the State Conference might be a substitute acceptable to both left and right, even though it was to have no legislative function. The some 2,400 delegates were carefully chosen to represent both conservative interests and the forces of "revolutionary democracy." The Bolsheviks refused to participate and helped organize an extremely successful general strike in Moscow on the day the conference opened. The contrast was instructive for the future: as businessmen, lawyers, trade unionists, politicians, and military representatives met inside the Bolshoi Theater to debate what course the state should follow, the workers of Moscow saw to it that stores were closed and transportation stopped; within ten weeks all the former groups were to be swept aside for good when the formal champions of the latter, the Bolsheviks, came to power.

The very representativeness of the State Conference foreclosed any possibility that it could promote unity. Political Russia at that moment was sharply divided between the right and the left, and so was the conference. The main result of the conference was to illustrate the extreme weakness and delicacy of Kerensky's position as he attempted to straddle the growing rift. The expected confrontation between Kerensky and Kornilov proved anticlimactic.

Kornilov appeared and was lionized but delivered a quite moderate address espousing his plans for strengthening the army. Kerensky gave a typically hyperbolic oration in which he warned against plots from either left or right and tried to placate both conservatives and socialists. In his closing address to the conference he became so carried away that he had to be applauded into ending his speech and nearly collapsed on the stage.

In retrospect, the most puzzling aspect of the State Conference is why Kornilov did not use the occasion to line up active and effective political support, at least behind the scenes, for his already prepared plan to restore order in Petrograd. A few days earlier he had arranged for two cavalry divisions to move to a point of concentration near Petrograd, and on the eve of the conference he told his chief of staff, General A. S. Lukomsky:

> It's time to hang the German supporters and spies, with Lenin at their head, and to disperse the Soviet . . . so that it would never reassemble. . . . I want to commit the leadership of this operation to General Krimov. I am convinced that he will not hesitate, in case of necessity, to hang every member of the Soviet.[7]

If these were his intentions, why didn't Kornilov seek a political base when he was in Moscow? First, because of his political inexperience he probably did not even consider it necessary to seek political backing for what he regarded as essentially a military action designed to clean out a nest of traitors and put some backbone into the government. Second, he may well have believed at this time that Kerensky supported his general ideas and would welcome a firm hand against the radicals in the capital.

Indeed, shortly after the Moscow State Conference ended, Kerensky did seem to be falling in with Kornilov's plans. He finally approved Kornilov's proposals for strengthening the army, and on September 5 he asked Kornilov to send a cavalry corps to

---

[7] Chamberlin, *The Russian Revolution,* I, p. 199, citing A. S. Lukomsky, *Vospominaniia* [Memoirs] (2 vols., Berlin, 1922), I, pp. 228, 229.

Petrograd. Kerensky, of course, was unaware that this was precisely what Kornilov was planning to do anyway, and he soon
regretted making the request. Apparently Kerensky asked for the
troops because he feared mass protests when the government began
to implement the sterner measures proposed by Kornilov. In the
meantime, Kornilov continued to plan a military move on Petrograd to take place September 9–14.

The affair now moved rapidly toward its confused denouement,
abetted by the bumbling intervention of V. N. Lvov, a self-
appointed intermediary between Kerensky and Kornilov. Lvov
(no relation to Prince G. Lvov, first prime minister of the Provisional government) had been a minister in an earlier cabinet of
the Provisional government. He undoubtedly had the best of intentions—and some were to conclude that he paved Russia's road to
hell with them. He apparently intended to strengthen the government by rallying conservative support to it. Hearing rumors of
plans being hatched around Kornilov, Lvov went to see Kerensky
on September 4; he urged the prime minister to broaden the government by adding representatives of right-wing organizations. He
also hinted broadly that he spoke for influential conservative
circles, though in fact he did not. Kerensky evidently encouraged
Lvov to find out more precisely what these circles had in mind.
Lvov later claimed that Kerensky had given him a wider mandate,
authorizing him to begin negotiations to broaden the government.

Lvov at once sought out Kornilov, telling the general that
Kerensky had sent him to ascertain what sort of government
Kornilov wanted. Kornilov, pleased at this overture from Kerensky,
said he desired the vesting of all power in the hands of the supreme
commander and a declaration of martial law in Petrograd; later
he made clear that the cabinet would also have to resign. He
warned Lvov that Kerensky was not safe unless the prime minister
came to headquarters. Kornilov clearly believed from what Lvov
had told him that Kerensky was ready to fall in with whatever
plans the general had.

This, of course, was hardly the case. When Lvov reported
Kornilov's demands to Kerensky, the prime minister was astounded

and frightened. Until then he evidently had believed that he could use Kornilov to further his own ends, but his plans never envisioned turning the government over to Kornilov nor Kerensky's own removal. To obtain confirmation of Lvov's report, Kerensky spoke directly to Kornilov in the conversation excerpted at the beginning of this section. Although Kerensky was deliberately evasive, suggesting only that he would come to headquarters the next day, Kornilov's affirmation that Lvov spoke for him convinced Kerensky that the general was preparing a bold bid to seize power.

Rejecting pleas that he clarify Kornilov's position directly with the general and that he attempt to work out some compromise, Kerensky met with the cabinet in the early morning hours of September 9 and explained the situation to his ministers. They promptly gave him full powers to deal with the danger, and Kerensky immediately wired Kornilov, dismissing him as commander-in-chief and ordering him to come to Petrograd at once. Kornilov refused to comply and was supported by the army commanders. Kerensky ordered the troop movements toward Petrograd halted, and Kornilov countermanded the order. The conflict was in the open, and there was little possibility of patching up the breach between the two men. A full-fledged counterrevolution had been launched.

Kornilov and his supporters were calm and confident. "No one will defend Kerensky. This is only a promenade," one of them reportedly said.[8] Nevertheless, several factors minimized their chances for success. First, they had not prepared the ground politically for their coup and thus had no significant organized support in Petrograd or elsewhere. Second, they mishandled the military maneuver itself, failing to provide proper communications and coordination for the advance on Petrograd. Third, the plotters were clearly acting in an illegal and undemocratic fashion; not only were they violating a basic prohibition among Russian officers against interfering in politics, they also were usurping state power by force. Kerensky was no longer very popular with anyone,

[8] *Ibid.,* p. 213.

either on the right or the left, and the Provisional government did not have much power or prestige, but he was the official leader of the nation and his government was the legal authority of Russia. For many the democratic regime in power, no matter how ineffectual, was preferable to a military dictatorship.

Finally, and most important, Kornilov and his cohorts failed to realize how fervently the Russian people as a whole believed in the mystique of the revolution and how actively they would resist any movement which seemed to threaten that precious symbol. In practice, as we have seen, the revolution had not fulfilled the particular aspirations of most individuals and groups, which was leading to mounting anger and disillusionment, but in principle the revolution still stood for liberation, hope, the promise of a better future. The fear of counterrevolution, of a return to the old repressions and injustices, served to rally the great preponderance of the population against Kornilov. Soviet historians have made much of the prominent role of the poorer classes in hastening to the defense of the capital and in turning aside Kornilov's troops— and indeed they played a key part—but it was not just the radicalized masses who defeated Kornilov, it was virtually all the citizenry, including moderates and even some conservatives.

In the rush to protect the revolution, the anti-Kornilovites had some powerful weapons at hand. Through the Soviet and the trade unions railway workers were instructed to hold up or divert the troop trains heading for the capital. Similarly, the telegraph workers were ordered to delay or not to transmit messages of the Kornilov detachments. Propagandists were sent to talk to the rank-and-file soldiers in Kornilov's divisions. The latter were urged not to risk their lives in an unworthy cause and were soon persuaded that what they were doing was both illegal and harmful to their own interests. In addition, forces in Petrograd were quickly mobilized to protect the city. Paramilitary workers' units, disbanded after the July Days, were now authorized as militia detachments and soon received arms. These detachments often fell under Bolshevik control and formed the nucleus for Red Guard units that later were active in the October Revolution.

As it turned out, Petrograd did not need to be defended. Between September 10 and 12, as the troops Kornilov had ordered to march on Petrograd neared the capital, the whole affair ended without a shot being fired and with barely a whimper. The soldiers sent to arrest Kerensky and the Petrograd Soviet were surrounded in the towns and at stops along the railroad line by Soviet representatives and local soldiers and workers: "Comrades, Kerensky freed you from the officer's stick, gave you freedom; and do you want to crawl before the officer again?" "Kerensky is for freedom and the happiness of the people. Kornilov is for discipline and the death penalty. Are you really for Kornilov?"[9] Before long Kornilov's divisions refused to go farther or they melted away; his forces simply disintegrated and the abortive counterrevolution was over.

Kerensky made himself commander-in-chief and sent the respected General Alekseev to headquarters to arrest Kornilov and his aides. They were treated surprisingly leniently. They were detained in a monastery in a nearby provincial town while the affair was being investigated. The investigation was not yet complete two months later when the October Revolution occurred. All the prisoners then escaped easily, most of them joining anti-Bolshevik forces in South Russia shortly thereafter. Kornilov himself was killed fighting the Bolsheviks during the civil war in 1918.

Soviet historians have alleged that the American and Allied governments secretly encouraged and assisted Kornilov but have produced little evidence to support this charge. Some Allied representatives in Russia were undoubtedly sympathetic to Kornilov's goal of restoring discipline in the army and at the rear, but official policy supported Kerensky and the Provisional government.

Although the Kornilov affair turned out not to be a serious danger to the government, its long-range consequences were immense. Kerensky was saved but had to rely on the Soviet and the masses to protect his government; they did not trust him, for his negotiations with Kornilov soon became widely known. He had alienated the right and the officer corps, who now despised him

[9] *Ibid.,* p. 219.

and would not lift a finger to help him. As Arthur Bullard, a young American correspondent in Russia at the time, wrote in his diary of the affair: "The outstanding thing . . . is that if Kerensky wins, it will mean that he has to rely on the Soviets. His evolution toward the Right is brought to an abrupt end."[10] Kerensky was dependent on the Soviet leadership and when the moderate socialists lost control of the Soviet and the Bolsheviks attained dominant influence with the populace, Kerensky had no place to turn for political support.

Although power did not actually pass to the Bolsheviks for two more months, the Kornilov affair sealed the fate of Kerensky's government. The vague fear of counterrevolution that had been bruited frequently in the preceding months had been made real and concrete. The one thing worse than conditions as they were was the prospect of going back, of returning to tsarist repression, of losing the Holy Grail of revolution. Although Kornilov's conspiracy had been flimsy, it gave everyone a whiff of that unacceptable possibility, and it provided Bolshevik propaganda with its most powerful weapon. Even those who wondered if the Bolshevik cry of peace meant selling out to the Germans and if the slogan "Land" led to illegal expropriation of property could be galvanized by the bogey of counterrevolution. It is doubtful that the Bolsheviks could have come to power some weeks later had they not been able to hark back to the specter of Kornilov and to pose as defenders of the revolution.

Although not directly implicated in the Kornilov affair, the Kadets must bear some responsibility for the erosion of the government's position that resulted from it. By standing aside and by endorsing conservative criticism of Kerensky, they contributed to the polarization of political Russia and to some degree encouraged the plotters. If the Kadets had acted vigorously, making common cause with the moderate socialists to oppose the Kornilovites, they might have dampened the movement before it became a threat. This would have undercut the fears of counterrevolution and per-

[10] Diary entry, 10 September 1917, Arthur Bullard Papers, Firestone Library, Princeton University.

haps given the Provisional government sufficient staying power to last until convocation of the Constituent Assembly at the end of the year.

Yet, looking back at the revolutionary crises of the summer of 1917, one is tempted to speculate that the most likely outcome for Russia was in fact counterrevolution and establishment of a military dictatorship. Of course, the Kornilov affair had its comic-opera aspects. Partly because of this and partly because it collapsed so ignominiously, most histories of the revolution imply that counterrevolution had little chance of success in 1917. This was not the case in my view. The effort centered on Kornilov was badly botched: Kornilov himself was monumentally ill-suited for his chosen role; his political advisers were pompous and incapable; his general badly mishandled the military maneuver against Petrograd; and the conservative forces in the country who supported him were neither astute nor courageous in their behavior. If at this crisis in the revolution there had appeared an able general and skillful politician who, like Napoleon, could have claimed to be defending the country and the revolution, and if the conservative politicians had acted vigorously and intelligently, the outcome might well have been different. Behind appealing and patriotic slogans and under effective leadership the soldiers might have been willing to suppress "traitors and German spies" in the capital. There would have been bloodshed and a brief civil war, but the force available to defend the Provisional government and the Soviet was untrained, unreliable, and limited. The crowds in Petrograd and Moscow could probably have been placated with promises and economic concessions and a firm military dictatorship established. Such a turn of events would undoubtedly have been fatal for the principles of the revolution and the nascent Russian democracy. But with that course not taken, the revolution now proceeded rapidly to a radical denouement.

6

The Vulnerability of the Provisional Government

★

It was a difficult meeting for both sides. Prime Minister Kerensky sat at his desk. Across from him were three leading moderate socialists, the Mensheviks Feodor Dan and A. R. Gots and the Socialist Revolutionary Nikolai Avksentiev. It was the evening of November 6, the very moment when the Bolsheviks were beginning their final bid for power. The callers urged Kerensky to proclaim at once a speedup in the meeting of the Constituent Assembly, the transfer of large landholdings to the land committees, and a proposal to the Allies for an immediate end to the war. Dan argued that only such action could "cut the ground from under the feet of the Bolsheviks." But the prime minister refused to do anything, apparently confident that he could crush any Bolshevik rising. He declared stubbornly, "The government does not stand in need of your advice."[1] Within a matter of hours Kerensky undoubtedly was wishing he had heeded their counsel.

Poor leadership was a serious liability of the Provisional government but far from its only one. The government emerged from the

---

[1] Quoted in Marcel Liebman, *The Russian Revolution,* trans. Arnold J. Pomerans (New York, 1972), pp. 224–225.

Kornilov affair tainted with counterrevolution, a suspicion that the masses continued to harbor. Moreover, it was politically weak, it failed to take more than halfhearted measures to meet the deteriorating situation, and it was unable to exert authority in the country as a whole. As in the February Revolution, the government was in part the engine of its own destruction. Not much of of a push from the Bolsheviks was needed; the Provisional government collapsed as much as it was toppled.

POLITICAL WEAKNESS

Inspired and powerful leadership would have been required to give the Provisional government even a modicum of a chance for survival. Yet it had no strong figures at all. Kerensky, emotionally and psychologically drained by the crises of the summer, seemed increasingly out of touch with reality and unable to cope with the pressing tasks at hand. Contemporary accounts suggest that he alternated between bouts of apathy and periods of breezy, defensive, and groundless optimism. On several occasions Kerensky seems to have concluded that he was doomed and that the moderate cause he led was hopeless, but on the very eve of the October Revolution he exuded confidence. He told a leading Kadet that he hoped the Bolsheviks would launch an uprising so that they finally could be smashed. He reassured the British ambassador along similar lines, and he announced to the public that the government was fully informed of all designs against it and that there was no need to panic.

Although some of this may have been whistling in the dark, Kerensky apparently really did believe that the Bolsheviks were much weaker and the government much stronger than each in fact was. This reflected his lack of political acumen and his gross misreading of the situation. When these faults were coupled with his conceit and obstinacy, he made a very poor leader indeed at this climactic moment for the government. Whether anyone could have done much is of course a moot point. Even a decisive, powerful figure would have had trouble reversing the rapid decline in the Provisional government's fortunes. But determined, vigorous leadership might at least have made the Bolsheviks' task harder.

A major weakness of Kerensky's government was that it included such a broad spectrum of political forces to the right of the Bolsheviks. Probably correctly, Kerensky had tried since spring to retain for the government the backing of both the non-Bolshevik socialists and the liberal Kadets. This was certainly the broadest base on which the government could rest. But by fall several glaring weaknesses of such a strategy had been revealed. First, the very breadth of the coalition made it almost impossible for the cabinet to take decisive action. The Kadets, who represented professional and business interests, vetoed radical policies and measures of social reform. At the same time, socialists opposed Kadet efforts to restore law and order and to pursue the war more vigorously. Constantly trying to appease both sides, Kerensky ended by accomplishing little. Moreover, the partners of the coalition increasingly distrusted each other, especially after the Kornilov affair. The socialists suspected that Kadets had connived with Kornilov, or at least acquiesced in his designs. The Kadets feared that the socialists were about to hand private landed property over to the peasants, to pull out of the war, and to dismember Russia among the national minorities. Finally, the two major groups on which the government relied were, by the fall of 1917, quite unrepresentative of the mass of the population. Neither the liberals nor the moderate socialists possessed the power and influence to undergird a vigorous and effective government; the Kerensky cabinet rested on past shadow not present substance.

In retrospect, we can speculate that an all-socialist cabinet might have been stronger, more viable. Yet in early October, as Kerensky laboriously glued together another coalition cabinet, he undoubtedly had some reservations about such a possibility. If the Kadets were left out, would this not permanently alienate the right, accelerate the political fragmentation of the country, and perhaps open the way to civil war? And what would it do to the war effort? Would the industrialists cooperate in maintaining production? Would the generals and officers continue to fight? To a considerable degree the war drove Kerensky, as it had leaders in other belligerent countries, to form a broadly based government, a government of "national unity," which might rally the nation in the desperate struggle against its enemies. The fact that the conservative forces in the country no longer trusted Kerensky was probably immaterial; at least for the moment they were not in open opposition, as they might well be if an all-socialist cabinet were formed.

In any case the government, which even as a coalition relied heavily on socialist support, was much weakened by the rapid erosion of the strength of the moderate socialist parties during the summer and fall. The Socialist Revolutionaries (SRs) polled the largest number of votes in the elections to the Constituent Assembly (finally held some weeks after the Bolsheviks came to power), but this plurality stemmed largely from traditional peasant identification with the SRs and masked some basic weaknesses. The leadership of the party was badly split among right, center, and left groupings. This greatly hampered both day-to-day practical operations and the formulation and propounding of major policy positions. By September the Left Socialist Revolutionaries (Left SRs) were virtually a separate party, cooperating fully with the Bolsheviks on most issues and entering the first Bolshevik-organized Soviet government after the October Revolution.

In addition, the Socialist Revolutionary program was rather general and fuzzy. As the situation deteriorated in the fall of 1917, large segments of the population were demanding more concrete plans and turned willingly to the specific promises of the Bolsheviks. Finally, the Bolsheviks were not in the least hesitant about adopting important parts of SR doctrine. In particular, Lenin, on coming to power, took over the SR position on the land problem (to distribute it to the peasants) and made it an effective plank of Bolshevik policy.

The Mensheviks, too, were split, though perhaps not as deeply as the SRs. Opposed to the moderate majority leadership was a more radical wing led by Iulii Martov. Moreover, an important component of Menshevik strength had always been the more skilled workers and the trade unionists in the labor movement. But in 1917, as these more settled proletarians were overwhelmed by the increasingly radicalized groups of unskilled workers and angry soldier-peasants, Menshevik influence among the masses dissipated rapidly.

The Mensheviks particularly, but the SRs as well, were further weakened in early fall by sharp differences over whether the new cabinet that Kerensky was forming should again be a coalition with the Kadets or an all-socialist government. Radicals in both parties, reflecting the popular mood and anxious to capitalize on the reaction against Kornilov, wanted to exclude the liberals and any other representatives of the "propertied classes." But the moderates, fearing the polarization of the country and aware of the risk of civil war, believed the partnership with the Kadets had to be reestablished. To have done otherwise would have meant repudiating the course the moderate socialists had pursued since spring and rejecting their ideological conviction that the revolution was in a bourgeois, not a socialist, phase. This they could not do.

Finally, both the Mensheviks and the SRs suffered from their association with the Provisional government, no longer popular with anyone, and from their dogged adherence to policies the majority of the people no longer supported. The growing numbers whom the revolution had failed to satisfy increasingly blamed the Mensheviks and SRs for that failure. Ever since the July Days, when the Menshevik and SR leaders had refused to accept power, the radical masses had had little faith in them. Now as the situation worsened and the parties stuck to the government and supported its unpopular positions on the war and land reform, the Mensheviks and SRs became thoroughly discredited. The moderate socialist leaders continued to exhort the people, but few were listening. As late as September 30 the newspaper of the Petrograd Soviet, *Izvestia* [News], which the Mensheviks and SRs still controlled, published the following appeal:

The government cannot possibly accede [to the popular demands] . . . Its prime task is to protect the entire nation, to save it from utter ruin, and to that end it can only pursue one path: to deny these demands, however just and well-founded they may be, and to impose sacrifices on all parties.[2]

But the Russian people were in no mood to make further sacrifices, and the Bolsheviks were prepared to fulfill the demands of the masses. Only on the very eve of the October Revolution did the moderate socialist leaders finally realize this—a bit too late.

Thus right up to the last few days of its life the Provisional government plodded suicidally along the path it had marked out for itself seven months previously. It continued to insist on prosecution of the war although even Kerensky angrily protested to the Allies in early October when they criticized the sagging Russian war effort. On another occasion he stated publicly that the Russian people were exhausted and the Allied armies would have to carry more of the burden. But in part because both Kerensky and the moderate socialists had great (and false) hopes that a conference of the Allied powers scheduled for Paris in early November might approve the opening of general peace negotiations, neither the government nor the Soviet leaders directly grasped the nettle of the war.

So it was also with the land issue. The most authoritative body representing the peasantry, the executive committee of the Congress of Peasant Soviets, proposed in October that pending final action of the Constituent Assembly, the government should transfer all private estates to the land committees. But the government took no action on this proposal and the peasants, who had already seized most of the land away, were delighted to believe in the Bolshevik pledge that they could keep it.

DESPERATION MEASURES

The Provisional government failed to act on the two most decisive issues—peace and land—but it was not totally paralyzed. In the last two months of its existence it took a number of sub-

[2] *Ibid.,* p. 226.

sidiary measures in a futile effort to strengthen its position. In keeping with Kerensky's strategy of balancing between right and left, some actions pleased the conservatives, some the socialists. The government also formed a representative advisory body which, had it been organized earlier, might have been quite helpful.

In steps which the right applauded, the Provisional government disbanded radical soviets in such cities as Tashkent and Rostov and permitted investigation of the Kornilov conspiracy to proceed in a lackadaisical way. The government was also able to stave off a threatened nationwide railway strike and to end serious strikes in the industrial Donets region. On the other hand, it won the approval of the left when it banned several extremist organizations involved in the Kornilov affair and forbade members of the Duma to meet, even as a private body. The government also abandoned Kornilov's scheme to militarize industry, which it had approved earlier in principle, and in no case did it apply the reinstituted death penalty at the front.

The most important measure the government took was an effort to rally political support by setting up representative bodies to exist until the Constituent Assembly could be convened. The first was the Democratic Conference, which met on September 27. Unlike the Moscow State Conference of the preceding month, the Democratic Conference excluded representatives of the right. Its some 1,200 delegates came from the soviets, from trade unions and cooperatives, and from various city and district bodies. It included an outspoken Bolshevik faction that harassed Kerensky and harangued the delegates at every opportunity. Although the body was undoubtedly broadly representative of the "revolutionary democracy" of Russia, it was unable to provide much concrete help to the government.

The most pressing issue before the conference was formation of a new cabinet; Kerensky had been carrying on with a rump cabinet since the resignation of the Kadet ministers during the Kornilov affair. But the conference soon found itself hopelessly divided on this question. Kerensky and his supporters favored a renewal of the coalition with the Kadets, as we have seen, but many members of the conference were opposed on the ground that some Kadets had been in sympathy with Kornilov. In a close vote, the Democratic Conference approved the idea of coalition; yet almost immediately it narrowly passed an amendment stating that the Kadets should be kept out of any coalition. Since the Kadets were the only significant nonsocialist party, the recommendations canceled each other. Unable to obtain clear guidance from the conference, Kerensky then proceeded to form a cabinet of his own, including two Kadets and a non-party businessman.

The Democratic Conference was superseded by the Council of the Republic, often referred to as the Pre-Parliament. It was a smaller and more influential body designed to act in an advisory capacity until the Constituent Assembly could meet. Convened on October 20, only a little more than two weeks before the October Revolution, the Pre-Parliament included the best of Russia's political leadership and public figures. Of its 550 members, some 80 came from the Democratic Conference, about 120 represented the propertied classes, 20 were Cossacks, and most of the rest were socialists. In terms of parties, there were about 120 SRs, 90 Mensheviks, 75 Kadets, and 65 Bolsheviks. The Bolshevik leadership at first approved Bolshevik participation, despite Lenin's vehement objections; but when the Pre-Parliament met, the Bolshevik delegation, led by Trotsky, staged an ostentatious walkout. Trotsky pointed out the helplessness of the Pre-Parliament and then lambasted the government:

The Provisional Government, under the dictation of Kadet counterrevolutionists and Allied imperialists, without sense, without force and without plan, drags out the murderous war, condemning to useless destruction hundreds of thousands of soldiers and sailors and preparing the surrender of Petrograd and the throttling of the Revolution. . . . We, the delegation of Bolsheviki, say: we have nothing in common with this Government of treason to the people and with this Council of complicity in counterrevolution.[3]

[3] Quoted in William Henry Chamberlin, *The Russian Revolution, 1917–1921* (2 vols., New York, 1935; reprinted 1965), I, pp. 283–284.

Although the departure of the Bolshevik faction should have facilitated the proceedings of the Pre-Parliament, that body accomplished little in the short span of its existence. There were long debates about how to resuscitate the army and how to persuade the Allies to agree to general peace negotiations, but in fact there was no chance of achieving either of these goals. Desertions continued to thin the army's ranks and no will to fight remained, while the Allies were more determined than ever to press the war to a victorious conclusion.

At first the Pre-Parliament also found itself stymied on political issues. Some members proposed that the body be given limited legislative authority and that the cabinet be made responsible to it. Kerensky's strong opposition soon scuttled this plan. As the political crisis deepened, however, and rumors of a Bolshevik takeover spread, the Pre-Parliament finally, at the eleventh hour, took a firm stance. The day before the October Revolution began, the Pre-Parliament endorsed (by 123 to 102 with 23 abstentions) a moderate socialist resolution that called for new policies on the part of the government, as we shall see in the next chapter.

DISINTEGRATION OF AUTHORITY

The Provisional government had never been able to exert full control over the vast Russian Empire, but in its final weeks the authority of the government dissipated rapidly. Power was slipping from its grasp not only in national minority areas and provincial cities and towns but also in peasant villages and districts and within the army. This meant that when the Bolsheviks seized power in Petrograd there was no group or region on which the Provisional government could rely for support.

By the fall of 1917 nationalist sentiment in the non-Russian areas of the old empire had gained considerable momentum. At the urging of national minority leaders the Provisional government permitted formation of special national units in the army. Thus there were soon Latvian, Ukrainian, Georgian, and other detachments, whose enthusiasm for the government was minimal. A national Muslim movement had considerable influence, while in

Central Asia tension between Russian colonists and local peoples paralyzed the government there. Finnish disaffection was intensified when, pressed by the Kadets, Kerensky dissolved the Finnish parliament and proposed a reduction in the considerable autonomy which the socialist leadership of the previous parliament had claimed. The government also exerted pressure on the Ukrainians in an effort to check the growing separatist tendencies there. But the tide of national liberation could not easily be stemmed, and the Bolsheviks, too, soon after taking power, found themselves obliged to swim with it.

Even in Russian areas the authority of the government eroded rapidly during the fall of 1917. For a few brief weeks at harvest time the supply situation improved and living conditions in the cities brightened a bit. But this was a temporary phenomenon and by the end of October food and fuel shortages were again widespread. Rioting and looting took place in a number of towns, and there was little the government could do to maintain order. Strikes occurred in many industrial centers, and local soviets, many of which had passed to Bolshevik control, began to encroach boldly on the prerogatives of the legal government. For example, on November 5 the Moscow Soviet extended its jurisdiction to local factories and declared itself the final arbiter of the hiring and firing of all workers. The Tiflis Soviet seized a printing press, set the local bread ration, regulated working conditions, and investigated suspected counterrevolutionaries.

This erosion of authority in the towns and cities was a serious blow to the Provisional government. Nevertheless, the decisive areas of its weakness were among the peasantry and in the armed forces. If the peasants had supported the government, Kerensky could have retreated to the countryside after losing control of one or more major cities and carried on the struggle. In the face of peasant opposition the Bolsheviks could not have retained and consolidated power after seizing it in Petrograd and other urban centers. During the subsequent civil war, peasant disenchantment with the Bolsheviks was what permitted anti-Bolshevik forces to continue the fight for so long.

Another serious blow to the Provisional government was the disaffection of the army. Despite Bolshevik influence among the Petrograd garrison and scattered units elsewhere, the existence of loyal troops in various parts of the country would nevertheless have made it possible for the government to campaign against the Bolsheviks after being displaced in Petrograd. With any substantial armed force arrayed against them, the Bolsheviks would have had a hard time holding on to power.

Moreover, it was not so much that the Bolsheviks won the soldiers and the peasants over as that the government lost them through its refusal to change policy on either the war or land reform issues. To permit a Bolshevik victory, it was not necessary for the great masses of Russia outside the cities and in the army actively to support Lenin and his followers; they had only to be passive, not to back or assist the government.

The great peasant rebellion discussed in Chapter Four was reaching its climax in the fall of 1917, particularly after the crops were harvested. The peasants then had plenty of time and energy to take over the landlord's land and property. The wait-and-see attitude that many peasants had adopted during the first few months of the revolution had gradually but sweepingly changed during midsummer into a resigned conviction that the Provisional government would do nothing. A grim determination to take matters into their own hands soon followed. In a vain attempt to halt this tidal wave of expropriation the government arrested some leaders of peasant violence in July and August and here and there was able temporarily to hold up the rush toward anarchy. But by October the flood was engulfing the whole of the countryside in Central Russia and in some other areas as well, and there was literally nothing the government could do about it.

In many places the peasants began by refusing to pay rent and by taking the landlord's wood or using his pasture. Most often this passed over to a seizure first of uncultivated then of all the landlord's land. Frequently the land was transferred to the local land committee (originally encouraged by the government) for redistribution among the peasants according to such traditional norms as size of the family and extent of existing holdings. Occasionally there was resort to violence, the burning of manor houses, and, more rarely, the killing of landlords and managers. Though it was a far-reaching social revolution, it was not in fact particularly bloody—mainly because nothing could resist this elemental drive of millions of Russia's long-suffering "dark people." A vivid eyewitness account by an owner's daughter of what happened to a private estate in the province of Riazan captures the spirit of the times:

> At midday the village assembly met to decide the fate of our property. . . . The question to be decided was posed with stark simplicity: should they burn the house or not? At first they decided just to take all our belongings and to leave the building. But this decision did not satisfy some of those present, and another resolution was passed: to burn everything except the house, which was to be kept as a school. At once the whole crowd moved off to the estate, took the keys from the manager, and commandeered all the cattle, farm machinery, carriages, stores, etc. . . .
>
> [Later] a sailor appeared, a local lad who had been on active service. He insisted that they should burn down the house as well. The peasants got clever. They went off to inspect the house a second time. One of them said: "What sort of school would this make? Our children would get lost in it." Thereupon they decided to burn it down [the next day]. . . . The whole village assembled and once again the axes began to strike. . . . They chopped out the windows, doors and floors, smashed the mirrors and divided up the pieces, and so on. At three o'clock in the afternoon they set light to the house from all sides.[4]

The revolution on the land, essentially accomplished by the time the Bolsheviks took power, was not directed against the government in particular; it took place despite or regardless of the govern-

[4] Quoted in John Keep, *The Russian Revolution: A Study in Mass Mobilization* (New York, 1976), p. 211.

ment. The peasants simply ignored what the government wanted them to do—wait until the Constituent Assembly. Seeing that there was no force capable of stopping them, they went about what they considered their rightful duty, taking the land. Most peasants didn't oppose the Provisional government, they merely didn't care about it. Thus when the Bolsheviks told the peasants they could keep the land they already had seized, they were quite content to accept the Bolsheviks and certainly would not lift a finger to aid the downfallen Kerensky.

We have seen earlier that the Kornilov affair greatly assisted the Bolsheviks' rise to power by providing them with the powerful propaganda slogan, "Counterrevolution." Indirectly it also aided them by accelerating the demoralization of the army. After the Kornilov escapade all officers were suspected of counterrevolutionary proclivities, and their already tenuous authority was entirely dissipated. The great bulk of the soldiers and sailors, sick of the war, refused to fight and quite often even to obey. One of the most astute of the political commissars serving with the army, V. B. Stankevich, summed up the situation:

> The authority of the commanders was destroyed once and for all. The masses of soldiers, seeing how a general, commander-in-chief, had gone against the Revolution, felt themselves surrounded by treason on all sides and saw in every man who wore epaulettes [officer] a traitor. And whoever tried to argue against this feeling also seemed a traitor.[5]

A deteriorating supply situation in the army aggravated the soldiers' basic distrust of officers and the government and their growing disgust with the war. Although the army's needs had priority, by the fall of 1917 the troops began to experience serious shortages of food and clothing. On October 29 the government told a session of the Pre-Parliament that because of a lack of flour a number of army bakeries had had to close. It also transmitted a telegram from the commander of the Northern Front: "The most

[5] Quoted in Chamberlin, *The Russian Revolution,* I, pp. 236–237.

terrible autocrat—hunger—threatens the army." The last minister of war in the Provisional government, General A. I. Verkhovsky, reported on the eve of the October Revolution that the minister of food had said that only 7 million soldiers of some 9 million in the army could be fed. Moreover, in September only 26 percent of the necessary flour had been delivered to the fronts, only 50 percent of the meat, and there was insufficient footwear for the coming winter. Verkhovsky concluded that the army could no longer fight and recommended that the government pressure the Allies for an immediate opening of peace negotiations. Kerensky responded by placing the outspoken general on leave of absence. Three days later the Provisional government fell.

Increasing violence accompanied the demoralization of the army. Officers were deposed, arrested, and sometimes shot. Mutinies and military riots occurred, which inflamed civilian disorders and anarchy. Stankevich summed up the impossible problem the Provisional government faced:

> The Stavka [army headquarters] was occupied with the problem of maintaining public safety in the rear and in the whole country. News continually arrived of terrible robberies, pillaging of estates, demolition of railroad stations, etc. No measures yielded positive results, because the troops on guard were as unreliable as the troops which committed the disorders, and often themselves took part in the rioting.[6]

Although the Military Organization of the Bolsheviks published its own paper, sent agitators to the front, and had active cells in a number of units, these efforts merely reinforced a process of decomposition in the Russian armed forces that would have taken place regardless as long as peace was not declared. As the army fell apart, the soldiers did not necessarily become Bolshevik activists, but they definitely rejected the government and its war policy. Thus when the Bolsheviks came to power in Petrograd, Kerensky had no reliable troops to turn to; the army was largely passive and neutralized.

[6] *Ibid.*, p. 238.

Could the government have done anything to cope with the mass revolution on the land and in the army? Certainly no secondary measures or minor shifts of policy could have stemmed the tide. A unilateral declaration of peace and the immediate transfer of land to the peasants would perhaps have saved the government temporarily. But patriotism and a sense of obligation to the Allies prevented the former, and an honorable but suicidal commitment to genuinely democratic decision making blocked the latter.

And what if the government had not changed its policies but there had been no Bolsheviks on the scene? Probably Kerensky and his ministers could have staggered along for a few more weeks or even months, but the disintegration of authority would have continued and the situation would have approached complete anarchy. The Bolsheviks, however, provided a ready and popular alternative to the Provisional government.

THE GROWTH OF BOLSHEVIK INFLUENCE

The Bolsheviks' rise to a place where they could assume power from the tottering government was meteoric. From being an extremist splinter group that many considered out of touch with reality, the Bolsheviks developed in seven short months into an influential, well-organized party capable of seizing and holding power.

The curve of Bolshevik ascendancy can be plotted in several ways. One is the size and extent of the party organization. From some 20,000 members in March the ranks swelled to about 260,000 on the eve of the October Revolution. Party committees grew from about 50 to 163 in the same period. Starting with one paper in March, the Bolsheviks were publishing 41 papers and journals in 320,000 copies a day by the end of August. In addition, Bolshevik representation in populist organizations such as factory committees and soldiers' committees had grown enormously.

Another measure of increasing Bolshevik strength was the results of elections to various city and district bodies. For example, on September 2 they won about 33 percent of the votes in elections to the Petrograd City Duma compared with about 20 percent they had received in district council elections in Petrograd in May. In Moscow the Bolsheviks soared from 11 percent of the vote in July to 51 percent in October in district council elections. In August, in the industrial town of Ivanovo-Voznesensk, the Bolsheviks won four-fifths of the seats in the Municipal Duma. It is important to note that these elections were open to all citizens of voting age. Clearly a growing proportion of the total urban population, not only the workers, was attracted to the Bolsheviks.

The key institutions in the Bolshevik climb to power were the soviets, and Bolshevik dominance in these bodies signaled the beginning of the last act of the revolutionary drama. On September 18 the Bolsheviks won a majority in the Moscow Soviet, five days after they had accomplished the same feat in the Petrograd Soviet. The central executive committee of the First All-Russian Congress of Soviets remained in the hands of the Menshevik-SR leadership, but the September victories of the Bolsheviks in the Moscow and Petrograd soviets meant that the Bolsheviks now exerted great influence in these two vital bodies. As a result, the Bolsheviks were able to press hard for convocation of a Second All-Russian Congress of Soviets, which they expected (correctly as it turned out) to be able to control and which was an essential element in their bid for power. Moreover, as the majority party in the two city soviets, the Bolsheviks could both use the resources of each soviet in organizing their insurrection and identify themselves with the concept "All Power to the Soviets." The trend toward the Bolsheviks was not limited to soviets in the two major cities, however; soviets in a number of provincial centers and towns also passed into the hands of the Bolsheviks in September and October.

But these victories in governmental bodies and the soviets only reflected a profound change of sentiment in much of Russia. How were the Bolsheviks able to win over increasing segments of the population? Part of the answer, as we have seen, was simply the disintegration of the Provisional government and the revulsion against its policies among the peasants and military ranks. At the same time, the Bolsheviks provided a program that increasingly appealed to various groups in Russian society. They publicized their position with growing effectiveness through propagandists and agitators, by popular word-of-mouth, through informal meetings, through speeches at more formal rallies, and through brochures, journals, and newspapers. By the fall of 1917 there were few politically aware Russians who did not know the Bolshevik position, although there were undoubtedly many who did not thoroughly understand it or recognize its full implications for the future.

The five issues that bore the Bolsheviks to power were peace, land, bread, workers' control, and fear of counterrevolution. By the fall of 1917 the patriotic feelings which the February Revolution had sparked had largely flickered out. As the hostile reaction among many to the humiliating peace treaty of Brest-Litovsk that Lenin was to sign with Germany in March 1918 showed, large numbers of Russians could not stomach surrender to the hated Germans. But the Bolshevik call for peace in 1917 was not couched in terms of a separate and abject acceptance of German terms. The Bolsheviks spoke of a general peace forced on all the imperialistic belligerents by their war-weary peoples. Though this was unrealistic in the extreme, most of the Bolsheviks' listeners were too fed up with the war to think through such a slogan. For them it simply meant an end to the fighting and sacrifice, a return to more normal conditions, and a chance to reap the fruits of revolution. Moreover, even some who would have preferred to continue to fight alongside the Allies against the German menace at last realized that the Russian people and army were no longer able to wage war; they concluded that peace was the only alternative to ruin and anarchy.

Naturally, as we saw earlier, the peasants responded enthusiastically when the Bolsheviks told them to take the land and use it. Other parts of the Bolshevik plank on this issue the peasants simply ignored. They paid no attention to Lenin's recommendations that the long-range goal was socialized use of the land and that some of the larger estates should not be broken up but should be preserved as model collective and socialist farms. The peasants took the land, divided it, and welcomed the Bolshevik ascent to power as long as it did not interfere with the peasants' own arrangements on the issue most central to them.

"Bread" symbolized the yearning of both peasant and city dweller for an end to shortages, a return to more normal economic activity, and improved living conditions. The Bolsheviks were in fact quite vague about what they would do to provide food, fuel, and housing, restore transport, and revive the economy. Few people understood what socialization of the means of production meant or where it would lead. But all could believe in the Bolshevik promise that things would be better; it was hard to see how they could be worse.

The workers, in a spirit of growing anarchy and disgust, were taking over the factories. Though Lenin and other Bolshevik leaders were aware that industry could not be run permanently on such a basis, for the moment the slogan "Workers' Control" was effective in rallying proletarian support to the party.

Finally, we have already discussed how important the threat of counterrevolution was in drawing people to the Bolshevik banner. Whatever the revolution meant to each of them, hundreds of thousands of individuals came increasingly to believe that the Bolsheviks were the one group able to protect and defend the revolution.

By midautumn of 1917 it was apparent that the existing situation in Russia could not continue for long. The political weakness of the government, the ineffectiveness of its last measures, the rapid disintegration of its authority, and the upsurge of Bolshevik influence all pointed to the imminent collapse of the Provisional government. The October Revolution was not inevitable, because the Bolsheviks had to develop the will to act. But the demise of the Kerensky regime some time in the near future would have been hard to avert. It had failed, not so much because of bad men and bad policies—in fact many of its personalities were honorable and praiseworthy individuals and many of its policies were principled and well-intentioned—but because the stance its heritage and circumstances forced it to take was no longer acceptable to most Russians, made desperate by three years of losing war and made vengeful by three centuries of social and psychological injustice. A great moment in history had arrived—and Lenin and the Bolsheviks were prepared.

7

The October Revolution: The Bolsheviks Take Power

★

Several things were happening at once, none of them quite believable yet each reflecting an aspect of the virtually silent, almost bloodless transfer of power that was to transform modern history. It was late evening on Wednesday, November 7. Mists rose from the Neva River in Petrograd. The night was dark, the moon obscured by clouds. It drizzled occasionally. For hundreds of yards along the river stretched the impressive buildings of the Winter Palace, the headquarters of the Provisional government.

Across the river a few Bolsheviks scampered along the parapets of the immense Peter and Paul Fortress. To signal the launching of the final attack on the Provisional government, a red lantern was to be displayed at the top of the Fortress. This would indicate that its guns were ready to shell the Winter Palace. But as if in some farce, no one could find a suitable lantern and the guns had to be oiled before they could be fired. Soon, however, Bolshevik leaders made sure a lantern was procured and the guns readied. Following a blank shot from the cruiser *Aurora*, anchored downstream under revolutionary command, the shelling began. It inflicted little damage on the Winter Palace and affected the struggle for control of the Russian government hardly at all.

On the opposite side of the river, in the center of the city restaurants were open and the opera *Don Carlos* was playing to an enthusiastic audience. In the meeting room of the Petrograd City Duma, its leaders expressed dismay and anger at news that the ministers of the Provisional government were besieged in the Winter Palace. After some exhortatory statements, they decided to adjourn their session and march peacefully to the Palace to share the fate of their friends and political colleagues there. Bolshevik members of the Duma ridiculed the idea and refused to go along. With a mixture of dignity and bravado, several hundred Duma deputies and their supporters moved four abreast slowly down the main street of Petrograd toward the Winter Palace. Before long a Bolshevik patrol of sailors halted them. The demands of the Duma deputies to be let through were laconically refused. One sailor threatened to spank them; others urged them to go back quietly, which they soon did.

In the Palace itself the situation was confused and eerie. Bolshevik besiegers slipped through gates and windows, climbed over walls, and sneaked in through underground basements and corridors. At first most were apprehended and disarmed. But as the resolve of the few student officers, Cossacks, and members of the Women's Battalion protecting the government weakened and their ranks thinned through desertion, the tables were turned. The Bolshevik infiltrators began to capture the defenders or to talk them into surrendering. Later, at 2:45 A.M., the insurgents finally reached an inner room in the center of the Palace where the leaders of the Provisional government had been meeting off and on for many hours.

The cabinet ministers, determined to perform their last act in authority with dignity, seated themselves around the meeting table. The guards outside the door offered to resist the revolutionaries, but the ministers ordered them to avoid bloodshed and surrender peacefully. The door burst open and a slight, bespectacled man walked up to the table and said, "You are all under arrest." This was Vladimir Antonov-Ovseenko, one of the planners of the Bolshevik insurrection. Despite demands from some of his more aggressive and rowdy followers that the ministers be lynched, he formally registered his prisoners and then conducted them to imprisonment in the same Peter and Paul Fortress from which the delayed signal for attack had originally come.

The astonishing ease of the overthrow of the Provisional government has led to several different interpretations of this climactic moment in the Russian Revolution. Some have seen it as a skillful conspiracy by Lenin and his cohorts, planned and calculated as the final step in a fanatical drive for power. Others have argued that the Bolsheviks "lucked" into office, assisted by a series of fortuitous accidents and the unexpected and extensive ineptitude of their opponents. Still others have concluded that the Bolsheviks came to power because of their tactical and organizational flexibility and their ability to reflect and articulate the masses' fundamental aspirations. As so often in history, elements of each of these explanations ring true. The Bolshevik leaders, pushed by a determined Lenin, did organize and plan the insurrection. Good fortune and their opponents' weakness certainly helped them succeed. And for the brief period between mid-September and early December 1917, the Bolsheviks probably did speak for the majority of the politically aware population of Russia. An examination of the events surrounding the October Revolution will show how all these factors interacted to bring the Bolsheviks to power.

THE BOLSHEVIKS DECIDE

It is difficult to identify a precise beginning to the rush of events that culminated in the October Revolution. The radicalization of the masses had been progressing since late spring, with marked acceleration from the time of the Kornilov affair. After a brief rebound following the July Days, the fortunes of Kerensky and the Provisional government had been steadily declining. A few militant Bolsheviks had been urging an armed uprising for months, but the Sixth Party Congress in August had adopted a cautious wait-and-see policy. As late as early and mid-October most party leaders seemed opposed to precipitous action, content to await the outcome of the convocation of the Second All-Russian Congress of Soviets and the elections to the Constituent Assembly, both set for November. The revolution seemed to be poised at dead center.

Lenin altered all this. He was clearly the catalytic agent for the process of insurrection. Still in hiding in Finland to avoid arrest, he sharply changed his mind twice in the early fall, but ended convinced that the Bolsheviks must seize power as soon as possible. During the middle of September Lenin's mood and outlook were quite restrained and moderate, in contrast to his earlier radicalism. In several articles written between September 14 and 25, he favored further development of the revolution through peaceful agitation and organizational work and was even willing to accept a socialist government excluding the Bolsheviks as long as the Mensheviks and SRs broke cleanly with the Kadets and other representatives of the bourgeoisie.

At some point between September 25 and 27 Lenin completely reversed himself and began to call stridently for an immediate armed uprising. The reasons for Lenin's about-face are unclear, but in a recent study Alexander Rabinowitch speculates sensibly that Lenin may have been encouraged by news reports suggesting a leftward surge in the provinces and in the army and by his belief that revolutionary sentiment was growing in Europe.[1] In addition, Lenin apparently decided that to postpone insurrection would provide time for the counterrevolutionary movement to develop and would weaken Bolshevik influence among the urban masses, who already were impatient for action.

The urgency with which Lenin now advanced his views can be gauged through these excerpts from the first two letters he sent to his colleagues on the party Central Committee after he had changed his mind:

The Bolsheviks, having obtained a majority in the Soviets of Workers' and Soldiers' Deputies in both capitals [Petrograd and Moscow], can and *must* take state power into their own hands.

[1] Alexander Rabinowitch, *The Bolsheviks Come to Power: The Revolution of 1917 in Petrograd* (New York, 1976), p. 179.

[The Bolsheviks should] organize a headquarters of insurgent detachments, distribute forces, move the reliable regiments to the most important points, surround the Alexandrinsky Theater, occupy the Peter and Paul Fortress, [and] arrest the General Staff and the government.[2]

Quite naturally his party comrades were astounded to receive such inflammatory advice. One of them, Nikolai Bukharin, recalled, "We all gasped. Nobody had yet posed the question so abruptly. . . . At first all were bewildered. Afterwards . . . we made a decision."[3] That decision was not to circulate Lenin's letters, to keep only one copy, and to take steps to prevent workers and soldiers from starting an armed rising on their own.

Undaunted, Lenin continued to press for revolution. But the majority of the party leaders clung to a more moderate line, maintaining that they could consider a transfer of power only if it were planned to coincide with the upcoming Second Congress of Soviets. That timing would permit the Bolsheviks to capitalize on the broad support the soviets enjoyed among the bulk of the population. Most workers and soldiers, and even many peasants, considered the soviets the only legitimate organs of authority and would have viewed an independent all-Bolshevik government with suspicion and resentment. Party cadres were thus instructed to organize their work and agitation around the resurrected slogan "All Power to the Soviets" and to develop popular pressure to make sure that the Provisional government did not block the convocation of the Congress of Soviets and that the congress would meet as soon as possible.

Events, however, favored Lenin. Rumors persisted that the Germans intended to march on Petrograd—or worse, that the Provisional government was preparing to turn the capital over to the Germans—even though neither the Germans nor Kerensky ever had any such intentions. Living conditions in Petrograd and other urban centers continued to deteriorate. Prices maintained their

2 *Ibid.*
3 *Ibid.*, p. 180.

steady upward spiral, and thanks to the virtual collapse of the transportation system and the economic strain of trying to sustain the war effort, shortages of food, fuel, and materials grew apace. This meant that industrial production was slowed or halted, workers were laid off, and anger and tension among the city populations mounted. Defiance and disorder were widespread, as a leading newspaper noted on October 3, 1917:

An open revolt flares up in Tashkent . . .
A mutiny in Orel. . . .
In Rostov the town hall is dynamited.
In Tambovsk guberniya there are agrarian pogroms; experimental fields are destroyed, also pedigreed cattle, etc.
In Novgorod-Voynsk uezd zemstvo storehouses are looted. . . .
Gangs of robbers appear on the roads in Pskov guberniya. . . .
In Finland the army and the fleet disassociate themselves completely from the Provisional Government.
Russia is threatened by a railway employees' strike . . .[4]

In this atmosphere of growing radicalism, tension, and uncertainty, Lenin continued to urge the Bolsheviks to action. He moved to Petrograd in mid-October to be in a better position to keep in touch with developments and to pressure his colleagues. His persistence at last began to bear fruit. On October 23 he succeeded in arranging a secret strategy meeting of a dozen members of the Central Committee in a remote apartment in a working-class district of Petrograd. By the time everyone arrived, it was late evening. Face to face with most of his top lieutenants for the first time in many weeks, Lenin launched a long, fervent elaboration of the arguments he had been advancing in his recent writings. He maintained that the international situation was favorable for a Bolshevik uprising and that domestic conditions differed markedly from those at the time of the July Days. "Now the majority [of the

---

[4] Editorial in *Volia naroda,* translated in Robert Paul Browder and Alexander F. Kerensky (eds.), *The Russian Provisional Government 1917: Documents* (Stanford, Calif., 1961), III, pp. 1641–1642.

people] is with us," Lenin concluded, and "the political situation is fully ripe for the transfer of power."

The debate among the top Bolsheviks lasted much of the night. Most of this group was not concerned about whether to attempt to overthrow the government but about when and how it should be done. Only two leaders, Lev B. Kamenev and Grigory Zinoviev, strongly opposed Lenin. They doubted that the Bolsheviks commanded majority support inside Russia and that European workers would come to the aid of a proletarian revolution in Russia. Afraid that the government was still strong enough to put down a premature uprising, they urged that the party work instead for the strongest possible representation in the forthcoming Constituent Assembly.

When the issue finally came to a vote, the Central Committee, by 10–2, endorsed a resolution hastily drafted by Lenin:

> The Central Committee acknowledges that the international situation as it affects the Russian revolution . . . as well as the military situation . . . and the fact that the proletarian party has gained majorities in the Soviets . . . makes armed insurrection the order of the day.
>
> Recognizing that an armed uprising is inevitable and the time fully ripe, the Central Committee instructs all party organizations to be guided accordingly and to consider and decide all practical questions from this standpoint.[5]

Though the precise timing and circumstances were left open, the Central Committee had made revolution "the order of the day" and had set the party firmly on course toward insurrection.

It was a great personal triumph for Lenin. Moments in history when a single individual can shape the direction of events are rare indeed; this seems clearly to be one of them. Almost alone Lenin saw that the Bolsheviks' only chance was to act as soon as possible while most of the population supported the party or was at least neutral and before the masses tired of talk and resolutions

[5] Quoted in Rabinowitch, *The Bolsheviks Come to Power*, p. 206.

and slid into anarchy and chaos. Once convinced that the right moment was at hand, he had conducted, doggedly and skillfully, a hammering, insistent campaign to win over both party leaders and rank and file. At some point the party might gradually have moved to adopt a strategy of revolution, but it undoubtedly would have acted too slowly and the transfer of power would never have occurred. Lenin, by the compulsion of his arguments and the wearing pressure of his willful determination, forced the party to go where it had to go if it were to come to power.

PREPARATIONS AND REACTIONS

Yet there was still to be a good deal of debate and maneuvering between the decision of October 23 and the seizure of power two weeks later. Lenin, of course, continued to urge immediate action, pointing out that "hunger does not wait." He insisted that the party should not link the uprising to the Congress of Soviets since the convening of the latter might be delayed or even prohibited. He recommended instead a preliminary conference of soviets from Russia's northern region, which the Bolsheviks were certain to control and which was meeting soon, as the vehicle for organizing and legitimizing a Bolshevik seizure of power. A number of militant Bolsheviks were delighted with this suggestion and took preliminary steps to carry it out. But most leaders of local party units in the Petrograd region and among the city garrison believed more time was needed to prepare the uprising. They warned also that the masses were counting on the Congress of Soviets to settle the question of a new government and would not necessarily support an independent seizure of power by the Bolsheviks.

Moreover, contrary to some earlier interpretations of the October Revolution, the Bolshevik party was not cohesive and tightly disciplined at this time. Zinoviev and Kamenev did not hesitate to carry the minority position they espoused at the historic meeting of October 23 into the party press, into their speeches, and into informal conversation and lobbying among their comrades. Nor were they alone. Some leaders in Petrograd sympathized with their position, as did several prominent Bolsheviks from Moscow. Zinoviev and Kamenev warned that the government was still strong, the soldiers apathetic, and the chances of a workers' revolution in Europe slim. An immediate rising would probably fail, with grave consequences for the party and for the Russian and international revolutions. They urged an intensified peaceful buildup of the Bolsheviks' strength instead.

The arguments of the moderates certainly had some influence within the party. According to one memoirist, party members were heard to complain openly, "Lenin has gone crazy; he is pushing the working class to certain ruin. His armed insurrection will get us nothing; they will shatter us . . . and that will postpone the revolution for years and years to come."[6] Such reactions must have infuriated Lenin. He berated Zinoviev and Kamenev in the press and at meetings. He also tried, unsuccessfully, to have them ousted from the party.

As the debate intensified, a middle position began to emerge, with which Leon Trotsky was soon identified. It was not as clear-cut as the views of Lenin or the moderates, but it appealed to a wide range of party members. Trotsky and others argued that while more time was needed to prepare militarily for forceful action against the government, it would be a mistake to wait for the Constituent Assembly. The assembly would not be under Bolshevik control since the peasant majority of the country would vote heavily for the SRs. Thus the right moment to strike was when the Second Congress of Soviets convened. This would allow the new government to appear as the choice of the masses rather than a single-party usurper of power.

Most important of all, Trotsky insisted that the seizure of power be presented as a defensive action protecting the soviets and the people from reactionary forces. As we shall see, this was a key factor in the Bolsheviks' success. It meant that many citizens could be persuaded to believe not that the Bolsheviks were illegally overthrowing a democratic government but that they were righteously

[6] Quoted in Marcel Liebman, *The Russian Revolution*, trans. Arnold J. Pomerans (New York, 1972), p. 240.

V. I. Lenin delivering a revolutionary speech. *Sovfoto*

defending the revolution and freedom against the dark forces of counterrevolution. As radical Marxists and a party at the extreme left of the Russian political spectrum, the Bolsheviks had little chance to gain and hold power. As representatives of the workers', peasants', and soldiers' soviets and as selfless guardians of that mystical "revolution" to which nearly every Russian was devoted, the Bolsheviks were almost certain to win.

Despite the attractiveness of the tactics Trotsky propounded, an instrument of revolution was still needed. And here luck—and their opponents—played into the Bolsheviks' hands. Just as the debate within the Bolshevik party was heating up, some of the leaders in the Petrograd Soviet, both Bolsheviks and moderate socialists, became alarmed over rumors that army headquarters and the government were planning to take military measures without consulting the Soviet. Orders were being readied to transfer troops of the Petrograd garrison to the front, it was said, and stringent steps were being planned to defend the capital against the Germans, who had recently captured Riga in Latvia as well as some islands in the Baltic Sea that guarded the naval approaches to Petrograd.

Consequently, on October 22, the Mensheviks in all innocence proposed in the executive committee of the Petrograd Soviet formation of a special committee to evaluate the capital's defense needs and to review movements of garrison troops with the military authorities. It was clearly a measure designed to assist the government by providing Soviet cooperation in the effort to counter further German advances. After brief discussion, however, the Bolshevik representatives turned this modest proposal into an antigovernment and semirevolutionary proposition which, approved several days later by a plenary session of the Petrograd Soviet, established a Military Revolutionary Committee (MRC) charged with determining the minimum forces that should remain in Petrograd, taking stock of personnel and weapons in the capital, and preparing a plan for the defense of the city. The intent was still clearly defensive, not insurrectionary, but the MRC was soon to become the center for planning the Bolshevik seizure of power.

The Mensheviks and right-wing SRs refused to appoint representatives to the committee, leaving its direction to the Bolsheviks and their allies, the Left SRs. A Left SR chaired the MRC, but the guiding force was Trotsky, now chairman of the Petrograd Soviet (as he had been twelve years earlier in the Revolution of 1905). Thus the MRC, ostensibly an arm of the Soviet, not of the Bolshevik party, was charged with defending the masses and the city of Petrograd against the Germans and counterrevolutionaries. In the process it served readily as the staff needed to organize a Bolshevik-led armed uprising against the Provisional government.

From this moment, Trotsky's role in the October Revolution became central. He emerged as the chief inspirer, organizer, and manager of the insurrection. To these tasks be brought formidable talents. Already a legendary figure because of his activity in the Revolution of 1905, he was a rousing orator and crowd pleaser. On several crucial occasions the force of his enthusiasm, personality, and words won over wavering groups of soldiers or workers. In addition, Trotsky understood that the specific steps toward seizing power must be carefully prepared and efficiently managed. His energy and skill ensured that the various Bolshevik efforts were coordinated and timed correctly. Trotsky's contribution to the Bolshevik victory has been subject to completely opposite interpretations: his followers have greatly exaggerated his role, while Soviet historians have denied it entirely, obliterating Trotsky from the pages of Soviet history. The fact is that Trotsky did a superb job in timing and administering the actual seizure of power, while Lenin provided the overall theory and the iron will needed to see it through.

The debates within the Bolshevik party and the fact that at least some Bolsheviks were intent on seizing power in the immediate future were no secret to informed Russian opinion. Kamenev published the results of the October 23 meeting of the Central Committee and his dissent therefrom in a Petrograd newspaper edited by the radical author Maxim Gorky. But several factors operated to blind people to the possibility of an insurrection and to smooth the Bolsheviks' path to power. First, many Petrograders preferred not to face reality and continued to act as if no political show-downs were looming:

> On the streets the crowds thickened toward gloomy evening, pouring in slow voluble tides up and down the Nevsky, fighting for the newspapers. . . . Mysterious individuals circulated around the shivering women who waited in queue long cold hours for bread and milk, whispering that the Jews had cornered the food supply—and that while the people starved the Soviet members lived luxuriously . . .
> Gambling clubs functioned hectically from dusk to dawn, champagne flowing and stakes of twenty thousand rubles. In the centre of the city at night prostitutes in jewels and expensive furs walked up and down, crowded the cafes.[7]

Second, the political groups that might have mobilized the greatest opposition to a Bolshevik coup, the Mensheviks and the SRs, found themselves in a difficult position. Since many of them were unhappy with the failure of the Provisional government to implement significant social reform or to embark on a bold policy to end the war, they had little desire to defend Kerensky. Yet they saw no clear alternative to the Provisional government. They feared that a Bolshevik attempt to overthrow Kerensky could only mean disaster for their own parties regardless of the outcome. If the Bolsheviks triumphed, the moderate socialists would be discredited and shut out. But if the Bolsheviks were defeated, the reaction against the attempted coup would destroy all socialist parties and Russia would undoubtedly suffer under the yoke of a military dictatorship. Thus they vacillated, urging decisive action on the government only at the eleventh hour when it was probably too late to deflect the Bolshevik drive for power.

Third, many people in Russia, beginning with Mensheviks and SRs and spanning the political spectrum to the extreme right, did not take a possible Bolshevik seizure of power seriously because they were convinced that it would be a temporary—even a health-

---

[7] Quoted in William Henry Chamberlin, *The Russian Revolution, 1917–1921* (2 vols., New York, 1935; reprinted 1965), I, pp. 295–296.

ful—aberration. Since the Bolsheviks were totally lacking in practical experience and had such extremist views, it was argued, they could not possibly run the government or put into effect policies that would work. Their regime would shortly fail, bringing hardship to everyone. Thus within a few weeks, or months at most, the people would be totally disillusioned with the Bolsheviks, sweep them out of office, and return to a more moderate political orientation. In this way the *narod* (the unlettered masses) would learn the emptiness of radical promises and be more willing than before to buckle down to the task of building a democratic, free Russia.

Finally, the Provisional government itself proved incredibly obtuse in the face of the clear threat from the Bolsheviks. The commander of the Petrograd Military District appears to have underestimated Bolshevik strength and exaggerated the forces on which the government could rely. Neither he nor the government set in motion the measures necessary to counter a revolutionary rising until it was too late. Worst of all, as we noted in Chapter Six, Kerensky, who dominated the government, alternated between despair and exuberance. The former resulted in apathy and inaction; the latter prompted overconfidence and boasting. To one of the Kadet leaders Kerensky asserted, "I hope to God that they [the Bolsheviks] start their uprising. I have more forces at my command than I need. They will be beaten once and for all."[8] This was less than a week before the Bolsheviks took power.

THE SUBVERSION OF THE ARMY

Although the forces involved in the October Revolution in Petrograd were small—a few thousand in a city of over a million citizens and garrison soldiers—the balance of military strength was crucial. In this regard two events turned the tide for the Bolsheviks. The first, occurring several days before the October Revolution, undercut the government's control over troops in Petrograd and made it impossible for the government to defend itself. The second, the inability of Kerensky and conservative generals after

[8] Quoted in Leibman, *The Russian Revolution*, p. 251.

the October Revolution to rally sufficient loyal troops for a counterattack, permitted the Bolsheviks to stay in power.

During 1917 the SRs had considerable strength in the army, mainly because most soldiers were peasants and the SRs were the party of the peasants. But as the young American historian John Bushnell has shown, the Bolsheviks as far back as the Revolution of 1905 had developed active and effective links to the armed forces.[9] During the World War and the summer of 1917 they increased their organizational and agitational work in the army and navy. This effort was to pay off richly in the days of their final drive to power.

As soon as the Military Revolutionary Committee became active, it developed close ties with garrison forces in Petrograd. The soldiers were in a restless and angry mood. In the period immediately preceding the October Revolution, the government had ordered a few thousand troops of some 200,000 in the city to the front (though the commander of the Northern Front had made clear that he didn't really want them because of their unreliability). The remainder of the soldiers were determined not to go to the front if they could possibly avoid it.

The MRC took two concrete steps to consolidate its influence in the garrison: (1) it sent its own commissars to act as liaison between the MRC and the various detachments and to replace commissars the Provisional government had earlier appointed; and (2) on November 3 and 4 it proposed to the headquarters of the Petrograd Military District that all orders to garrison units should be countersigned by MRC representatives. When the commanding general naturally refused the proposal, Trotsky distributed a statement openly repudiating the government's authority. After reporting briefly the rejection of the MRC demand, Trotsky asserted:

> In so doing, the headquarters breaks with the revolutionary garrison and the Petrograd Soviet. . . . The headquarters be-

[9] John Bushnell, "Mutineers and Revolutionaries: Military Revolution in Russia, 1905–07," (Ph.D. diss., Indiana University, 1977).

comes a direct weapon of counterrevolutionary forces. . . . The protection of revolutionary order from counterrevolutionary attacks rests with the revolutionary soldiers directed by the Militay Revolutionary Committee. No directives to the garrison not signed by the Military Revolutionary Committee should be considered valid.[10]

The government's inability to meet this insurrectionary challenge was in fact the turning point of the October Revolution, although the formal transfer of power took place two days later.

On November 4 and 5 the staff at military headquarters, recognizing that their flat denial of the MRC request had been a tactical mistake, initiated negotiations with representatives of the MRC and leaders of the garrison. The staff sought a compromise that would permit an MRC presence at headquarters without subverting the officers' authority. Under pressure from moderate socialists in the Soviet, the MRC finally rescinded Trotsky's declaration—but by then it was too late for the government. MRC commissars were actually in place and directing or strongly influencing unit decisions. The great majority of soldiers were no longer willing to obey the orders of the government or the military authorities unless the MRC said they should.

The significance of this decisive event in the history of the revolution is not that it added military forces to the Bolshevik side but that it denied them to the government. During the seizure of power on November 6 and 7, relatively few soldiers fought with the Bolsheviks. On the other hand, almost none did anything to defend the Provisional government. The overwhelming majority of the garrison troops were passive and neutral.

A good example of this phenomenon is the sequence of events at the Peter and Paul Fortress. This extensive complex of buildings, redoubts, and cannon, notorious as a prison for political prisoners under the tsars, was important to the insurrectionists on two counts: it commanded the Neva River and the Winter Palace, and it was a depot for large amounts of weapons and supplies. The

[10] Quoted in Rabinowitch, *The Bolsheviks Come to Power*, p. 241.

soldiers stationed there were considered supporters of the government, and some in the MRC had recommended besieging and storming the Fortress. But Trotsky urged that a frontal assault be delayed to let him appeal personally to the Fortress garrison.

Accompanied by a small group of comrades, Trotsky spent several hours on the afternoon of November 5 haranguing the troops inside the Fortress. Eventually most of them agreed to obey the orders of the MRC and not to oppose Bolshevik plans to distribute the arms in the Fortress and to use it in the final assault on the Winter Palace. But many members of the garrison refused to take any part in insurrectionary activity, and the gunners were so uncooperative in preparing the Fortress's cannon that Bolshevik naval gunners had to be brought in. The outcome, however, was the same as at many other places in the city during the October Revolution: a handful of Bolsheviks achieved a bloodless victory and no one lifted a finger to save the government.

ON THE EVE

Despite their success in securing the Peter and Paul Fortress and their mastery over most of the garrison, the leaders of the MRC still proceeded prudently on November 5—and for good reason. On the military side they had several worries. Though they believed that the bulk of the troops in Petrograd were passive or sympathetic, the MRC planners did not know exactly how strong the government forces might turn out to be, and they were well aware that their own numbers and equipment were limited. Further, they were unsure whether front-line soldiers might not be brought quickly to the capital and used against them. Even though some reports indicated that the troops at the front were as demoralized as those in Petrograd, the situation was by no means clear.

Moreover, even if they were successful in Petrograd, the revolutionary leaders had to consider whether people in the rest of the country, and particularly the peasantry, would accept a new government's self-proclaimed authority. If they did not, the Bolsheviks would soon find themselves isolated in the capital. Though there were fragmentary reports of a leftward swing of sentiment in a number of parts of Russia, the leaders in Petrograd had little definite information about the situation throughout the country.

Finally, even the attitudes of the Petrograd population seemed mixed. Conflicting evaluations were received at Bolshevik headquarters in the Smolny Institute. Some indicated that the workers were impatient for action and would wholeheartedly support an uprising; others suggested that the masses were uncertain and apathetic, that many people were sitting back waiting for the Congress of Soviets to solve all their problems.

Partly because of these concerns and partly because the MRC leaders skillfully hewed to their chosen tactical line of appearing to defend the Soviet and the people against the forces of counterrevolution, they were careful not to trigger the insurrection prematurely nor to appear to be directly attacking the government. This caution infuriated Lenin, who continued to insist that the Bolsheviks must take power *before* the Congress of Soviets convened. He considered it vital to present the Congress with a *fait accompli*; only in this way could the Bolsheviks be sure of controlling the new government.

As the tension mounted and the signs of an impending showdown multiplied, the government at last decided to act. On November 5 Kerensky, in a burst of energy and anger, proposed to his cabinet that the entire MRC membership be arrested. Anxious to avoid a direct confrontation with the Soviet, the ministers finally agreed on more limited steps: to initiate criminal charges against MRC members for inciting the population to revolt; to return to jail those Bolshevik leaders, including Trotsky, who were out on bail following their imprisonment after the July Days; to close two Bolshevik and two right-wing newspapers; and to order loyal troops from outside the capital to Petrograd.

In the early morning hours of November 6, a detachment of government troops seized the Bolsheviks' printing premises and posted a guard to prevent the press from being reopened. The MRC was quick to react. A few hours later it issued a proclamation to regimental committees and commissars in military units entitled "Directive Number One." Reporting that the Bolshevik papers had been closed and government troops were being assembled, it declared, "The Petrograd Soviet is in direct danger. . . . You are hereby directed to bring your regiment to battle readiness [and to] await further instructions."[11]

Following this near call to arms, Bolshevik leaders met to decide what to do next. Their indecisive discussions lasted all that day and into the night of November 6–7. The militants wanted to move immediately to an all-out assault on Kerensky; others were still reluctant to force an open clash with the government. Members of the Bolshevik Central Committee were assigned specific tasks considered necessary for a successful rising, such as ensuring the cooperation of the railway, postal, and telephone and telegraph workers and organizing a continued supply of food to the city. There was much talk about guaranteeing and defending the imminent convocation of the Congress of Soviets but no mention of an immediate insurrection or a direct attack on the government.

In the meantime, Trotsky and the MRC leaders were pursuing a policy of active defense, soon scoring several notable victories. During the morning of November 6, a detachment of soldiers under Bolshevik command was ordered to the printing plant, where they overwhelmed the government guards. Under revolutionary protection, the presses were soon running again. The same morning the government, aware that the crew of the cruiser *Aurora* was sympathetic to the Bolsheviks, ordered it to sea. But the MRC had the order countermanded, the crew mutinied, and the ship passed to Bolshevik control.

November 6 was a crucial day for the government, both militarily and politically. During the morning Kerensky tried to reassert the government's authority over the garrison. This failing, he then pinned his hopes on the arrival of loyal troops from outside the city. As the day wore on, however, it became clear that such reinforcements would be few and slow in coming. Most of the commanding officers were in no hurry to help Kerensky, who had angered some of them and who seemed weak and erratic to others. Moreover, units that set out toward Petrograd were de-

---

[11] Quoted in Rabinowitch, *The Bolsheviks Come to Power*, p. 249.

layed or blocked by the agitation of bolshevized soldiers and workers, by the sabotage of their transport and communications by radical railwaymen and telegraph operators, and by the general confusion and chaos that existed in the region between Petrograd and the front lines. By the end of the day the government had been able to muster only about 2,500 loyal troops, mainly officers, students in the military academies, and members of the Women's Battalion.

During the afternoon Kerensky appeared before the Pre-Parliament to seek its endorsement of strong measures against the insurrectionists. In a long, emotional speech, he called the Bolsheviks traitors and depicted action against them as a defense of freedom and the revolution, asserting that the Bolsheviks were aiding

> not the German proletariat but . . . the German ruling classes. . . . In full awareness of my responsibility I proclaim from this platform that such actions by a Russian political party constitute treason and a betrayal of the Russian state. . . . Those groups and those parties which have dared to raise a hand against the free will of the Russian people, threatening at the same time to expose the front to Germany, are subject to immediate, decisive, and total liquidation.[12]

To Kerensky's surprise, the Pre-Parliament did not back him. After debating the matter into the early evening, the majority of deputies rejected a policy of repression against the Bolsheviks, though condemning the latter's actions. Instead, they narrowly passed a resolution sponsored by Feodor Dan, a leading Menshevik, and other moderate socialists that called for radical reform on the issues of peace and land and establishment of a broadly representative committee of public safety to work with the Provisional government in restoring order. Dan and his supporters were convinced that the Bolsheviks could be stopped only by taking the wind from their sails through immediate announcement of a program that had popular appeal.

[12] *Ibid.,* pp. 256–257.

As we saw at the start of Chapter Six, Dan and two colleagues from the Pre-Parliament went at once to a cabinet meeting in the Winter Palace, hoping to persuade Kerensky to accept the resolution and to publish throughout the city that very night promises to open negotiations to end the war, to transfer land to the land committees, and to hasten convocation of the Constituent Assembly. But Kerensky was alternately enraged and made despondent by their unwelcome advice, finally dismissing them with the comment that the government has "no need for admonitions and instructions" and would "cope with the rebellion by itself."

The crisis was probably too far advanced and the populace too disillusioned with the Provisional government for Dan's last-minute prescription to have worked, but quick proclamation of reforms and of the opening of peace negotiations would certainly have increased the doubts about an uprising among Bolshevik moderates and perhaps brought some of the wavering garrison soldiers to the side of the government. Why Kerensky rejected Dan's advice is a mystery. By that time he must have sensed that the available forces were inadequate and that he badly needed new political support, even if it meant a radical policy change. Perhaps he still counted on loyal forces from the front coming to his rescue.

A last effort to undercut the Bolsheviks politically developed during the night of November 6 and the morning of November 7. Caucuses of Menshevik and SR delegations to the Congress of Soviets each agreed to explore the possibility of replacing the Kerensky cabinet with an all-socialist coalition government under the aegis of the congress. But it was really too late, and the final scenes in the Bolsheviks' drive to power were now played out.

THE OVERTHROW OF THE
PROVISIONAL GOVERNMENT

Late in the afternoon of November 6, the MRC took its first clearly offensive action when detachments under its control occupied the central telegraph office. At about the same time government authorities ordered three of the bridges across the Neva raised and the fourth secured by loyal troops to prevent revolutionary forces from the working-class districts and suburbs from reaching the central part of the city, where most government offices were located. This maneuver was only partially successful because the revolutionaries were able to prevent two of the bridges from being raised and then to put them under revolutionary guard.

Despite these first skirmishes and the quickening pace of revolutionary activity, life in Petrograd remained astonishingly normal. There were a number of meetings in factories and barracks to whip up enthusiasm among workers and soldiers but no mass demonstrations or gatherings of crowds on the streets. Streetcars ran almost as usual, and there was little disorder. The Russian writer Zinaida Gippius and her husband went out for a walk and observed that the day was gray and quiet. No one seemed to be paying much attention to a number of posters on the walls which proclaimed, "The Government has been overthrown."

In a sense this was the calm before the storm. Sometime after midnight on November 6–7, the revolutionary forces launched a thoroughgoing assault on the government. Unfortunately the historical record is not clear as to why the leaders of the MRC and the Bolshevik party decided definitely at this time to take the offensive. Perhaps the momentum of events and the enthusiasm of detachment commanders simply pulled them along. It is tempting, however, to speculate that Lenin, who had done so much to push the party toward revolution, also influenced this final irrevocable step. There is no direct evidence to support this hypothesis but the circumstances are suggestive.

Lenin, mostly confined to his apartment hiding place on the outskirts of Petrograd since his return to the city several weeks earlier, became increasingly impatient as the tempo of events quickened. He continued to urge immediate action before the opening of the Congress of Soviets, scheduled for November 7. As it became clear that his advice was not being taken, Lenin could contain himself no longer. Ignoring party discipline, he called on the rank and file, as he had done earlier when party leaders seemed to be turning a deaf ear to his exhortations. On the evening of November 6 he drafted an appeal to the city and district committees of the party urging the arrest of the government that very night. Several hours later, disobeying instructions of the Central Committee to remain in hiding, and with a warrant out for his arrest, Lenin set out via back streets for the Bolshevik headquarters at Smolny. After one scare as a government patrol passed nearby, Lenin arrived safely and immediately began to upbraid his colleagues, demanding action to arrest the government at once.

Whether his intervention was decisive can probably never be definitively determined; in any case, between 2 and 6 A.M. on November 7, forces of the Military Revolutionary Committee seized the post office, the main power station, and a bridge. Later in the morning they secured the central bank, the last of the railway stations in Petrograd (others had been captured earlier), and the telephone central (thereby cutting off most of the government's communications). Naval units from Kronstadt and Helsingfors (Helsinki) were ordered to converge on the capital, and plans for besieging the Winter Palace were drawn up.

The almost effortless way in which the Bolsheviks gained control of the city and the helplessness of the Provisional government as its authority and power slipped away were well summarized in a telegram on the night of November 6–7 from the commander of the Petrograd Military District to the commander-in-chief of the Russian army:

> I report that the situation in Petrograd is threatening. There are no street outbreaks or disorders, but a systematic seizure of institutions and stations and arrests are going on. No orders are carried out. The junkers [student officers] give up their posts without resistance. The Cossacks, notwithstanding a number of orders, have not come out of their barracks up to this time. Recognizing my full responsibility before the country, I report that the Provisional Government is in danger of losing its power.[13]

[13] Quoted in Chamberlin, *The Russian Revolution,* I, p. 315.

By the morning of November 7 Kerensky realized that the government's situation was desperate. He then decided to go personally to the headquarters of the northern armies at Pskov to round up loyal troops and bring them back to the capital. Since the revolutionaries controlled the railroad stations and the port, Kerensky and his assistants, after several hours of searching, requisitioned two suitable automobiles, one of them belonging to the American Embassy in Petrograd, and headed south at midmorning. An hour or so later revolutionary units dispersed the Pre-Parliament when it tried to reconvene. No deputies were arrested and there was no violence. Nor was there any resistance as this semilegislative institution of the old government disappeared quietly from the scene.

That same morning Lenin drafted a manifesto proclaiming the transfer of power to the Military Revolutionary Committee acting on behalf of the Petrograd Soviet. When the Soviet convened in early afternoon, Trotsky announced the overthrow of the Provisional government and Lenin spoke briefly. Neither paid any attention to comments from the floor that any transfer of power should await the meeting of the Congress of Soviets later that day.

As events moved toward a climax, Lenin's plans were nearly upset by a series of unavoidable delays and minor snags. As early as 1 P.M. revolutionary forces had surrounded and cut off the Winter Palace, where the cabinet (without Kerensky) was meeting. But the final attack kept being delayed, partly to permit further preparations for it, partly to overcome irritating problems like those at the Peter and Paul Fortress described at the beginning of this chapter, and partly to allow more time to persuade government forces in the Palace to surrender. Since Lenin was adamant that the ministers be arrested before the Congress of Soviets convened, the Bolsheviks kept maneuvering to delay the opening of the Congress, originally scheduled for 2 P.M.

At 6:30 P.M. on November 7, the MRC delivered an ultimatum to the government to surrender, but the cabinet decided to ignore it. Still the MRC leaders delayed, correctly calculating that in terms of the military balance of forces time was on their side. Though further postponement of the final assault made Lenin uneasy, it did help the besiegers of the government. As we saw at the start of the chapter, revolutionaries were able to infiltrate the Winter Palace, capturing some of the defenders and persuading others to give up. As the night wore on, the isolated and out-manned troops inside became increasingly demoralized, and by 10 P.M. about half of them had surrendered or slipped out of the Palace. The guns of the Peter and Paul Fortress, which began to shell the Palace around 11 P.M., did little damage but frightened the defenders still further. The last attempt to save the government was the gallant but futile effort of the Petrograd Duma deputies to reach the Palace that was recounted at the opening of this chapter. Around 2 A.M. the ministers were arrested, word of which was passed quickly to the anxious Bolshevik leaders at the Second Congress of Soviets. The Provisional government had fallen, and a major turning point in modern history had been reached. What had been the sacrifices in this momentous revolution?—a few dozen casualties in the siege of the Winter Palace and a few hundred in Petrograd as a whole.

THE SECOND ALL-RUSSIAN CONGRESS OF SOVIETS

By late evening on November 7, the opening of the Second All-Russian Congress of Soviets could no longer be delayed, and it was called to order at 10:40 P.M. Fortunately, the radical American journalist John Reed has left us a graphic and stirring eye-witness description of the scene:

> In the rows of seats, under the white chandeliers, packed im-movably in the aisles and on the sides, perched on every window-sill, and even the edge of the platform, the representatives of the workers and soldiers of all Russia waited in anxious silence or wild exultation the ringing of the chairman's bell. There was no heat in the hall but the stifling heat of unwashed human bodies. A foul blue cloud of cigarette smoke rose from the mass and hung in the thick air. Occasionally someone in authority mounted the tribune and asked the comrades not to smoke; then everybody, smokers and all, took up the cry "Don't smoke, comrades!" and went on smoking. . . .

On the platform sat the leaders of the old *Tsayee-kah* [Central Executive Committee] . . . Dan . . . was ringing the bell. Silence fell sharply, intense, broken by the scuffling and disputing of the people at the door.[14]

Three hundred of the some 670 delegates were Bolsheviks who, when joined by almost 100 Left SRs, commanded a majority in the congress. As a result, the old moderate socialist leadership, in power since the First Congress in June 1917, resigned to be replaced by Bolsheviks and Left SRs. The congress began its deliberations in a quite moderate and conciliatory vein. Iulii Martov, a radical Menshevik, proposed formation of a democratic government representing the interests of all the nonpropertied elements of Russia. This idea was warmly received by the deputies, and the Bolsheviks had no choice but to acquiesce in it. The tone of the proceedings soon soured, however, as other Mensheviks and right-wing SRs rose to denounce the Bolshevik usurpation of power. Angry rejoinders from the radicals followed.

At this juncture the Mensheviks and right-wing SRs made a serious tactical mistake. Instead of remaining to try to work out a compromise all-socialist government, or at least to harass and discomfit the Bolsheviks and their allies, they walked out of the congress, thereby giving the Bolsheviks free rein. A Menshevik participant and memoirist of the revolution, N. N. Sukhanov, incisively evaluated the effect of the withdrawal of the moderate socialists:

We completely untied the Bolsheviks' hands, making them masters of the entire situation and yielding to them the whole arena of the revolution. A struggle at the congress for a united democratic front *might* have had some success. . . . By quitting the congress, we ourselves gave the Bolsheviks a monopoly of the Soviet, of the masses, and of the revolution. . . . We ensured the victory of Lenin's whole "line."[15]

[14] John Reed, *Ten Days That Shook the World* (New York, 1935), pp. 86–87.
[15] Quoted in Rabinowitch, *The Bolsheviks Come to Power*, p. 294.

In fairness, it is important to remember that the moderate socialists considered the unilateral Bolshevik action both traitorous to Russia and totally unsocialist. Moreover, they were convinced that the Bolsheviks could not hold power and that the reaction to the coup would destroy them all. Their indignation and concern are fully understandable but their action meant that Lenin and his comrades had a clear field. In a fiery speech, Trotsky lost little time in making the break between the radical left and the moderates irreparable. He concluded his condemnation of the Bolsheviks' opponents by consigning them to "the trash can of history."

A few radical Mensheviks who remained and some of the Left SRs urged reconciliation with the departed socialists and offered to mediate the dispute. But the Bolsheviks were in charge and soon moved to formalize their assumption of power. They presented a manifesto written by Lenin and addressed "To All Workers, Soldiers, and Peasants." The heart of it read:

> Supported by an overwhelming majority of the workers, soldiers, and peasants, and basing itself on the victorious insurrection of the workers and the garrison of Petrograd, the congress hereby resolves to take governmental power into its own hands.
>
> The Provisional Government is deposed and most of its members are under arrest.
>
> The Soviet authority will at once propose a democratic peace to all nations and an immediate armistice on all fronts. It will safeguard the transfer without compensation of all land—landlord, imperial, and monastery—to the peasant committees; it will defend the soldiers' rights, introducing a complete democratization of the army; it will establish workers' control over industry; it will insure the convocation of the Constituent Assembly on the date set; it will supply the cities with bread and the villages with articles of first necessity; and it will secure to all nationalities inhabiting Russia the right of self-determination.
>
> The congress resolves that all local authority shall be transferred to the soviets of workers', soldiers', and peasants' deputies,

which are charged with the task of enforcing revolutionary order.[16]

At about 5 A.M. on November 8 the congress overwhelmingly approved this manifesto. The Bolsheviks, a tiny handful of extremists eight months earlier, were in power. As Lenin murmured to Trotsky the next night when the new government was confirmed, "It makes my head spin."

[16] *Ibid.,* p. 303.

8

The New Soviet State: Consolidating Power

★

THE REVOLUTION OUTSIDE PETROGRAD

By November 8 the Bolsheviks had overthrown the central government in Petrograd and controlled the capital. That same day they organized the first Soviet government and issued their first decrees. But the Russian Empire was vast, and whether they could retain power depended to a considerable degree on what happened in the rest of the country. Several particular danger spots existed: Moscow (the other major city and the old capital), the non-Russian borderlands, and the concentrations of troops at the front were all potential bases around which anti-Bolshevik forces might rally and from which a major attack on Red Petrograd could be launched. Moreover, it was hard to predict the attitude of the peasantry, traditionally considered a conservative force but acting in 1917 in a radical and anarchic manner.

At first the October Revolution spread slowly and sporadically to the rest of the country. A major struggle for Moscow took place. Reacting to the news from Petrograd, on November 7 the Moscow Soviet, under Bolshevik control since September, established a military revolutionary committee of its own. Moderate forces reacted just as quickly, however. The same day, on the initiative of members of the Moscow City Duma, a Committee of Public Safety was formed which pursued a vigorous policy in defense of the old government, working closely with the staff of the Moscow Military District. Both groups, each claiming to be the legitimate authority in Moscow, jockeyed for position on November 8 and 9.

As in Petrograd, the great majority of the army units in Moscow remained passive. The Bolsheviks' motley force was larger than that of the government, but its members were ill-trained and, at least in the beginning, it was rather disorganized. Bolshevik strength was mainly scattered in outlying districts, while the moderates held the center of the city. An exception was the Kremlin itself, the old fortress and religious and governmental center in the heart of Moscow. A pro-Bolshevik junior officer had won over the garrison there, but before long his forces were largely isolated. Government units seized a number of key points on the night of November 9, and the Bolshevik group in the Kremlin surrendered the next day.

Before long, however, the tide turned in the Bolsheviks' favor. Heavy fighting continued for several days, but on the afternoon of November 15 the Moscow Committee of Public Safety signed a peace agreement, dissolving itself and ceding authority to the local MRC. The revolution in Moscow had been won, at the cost of a thousand casualties and some damage to the Kremlin and other old buildings from artillery fire.

Several factors help to explain why the pattern of revolutionary events in Moscow differed from that in Petrograd. Moscow was traditionally a more conservative city, representing "old Russia," and its business and professional class was quite strong and active. The Bolshevik leadership in Moscow was more moderate than that in Petrograd and though they acted as soon as they heard of the insurrection in the capital, they lacked the enthusiasm and élan of their more militant comrades to the north. Moreover, the Moscow Bolsheviks had done little advance planning for a revolt and had no preparatory instrument like the MRC of the Petrograd Soviet to organize it.

Guarding Smolny Institute, headquarters of the Bolsheviks, during the October Revolution. *Bildarchiv Preussischer Kulturbesitz*

In much of the rest of the country the Bolsheviks were soon able to exert their authority, with the process occurring at different tempos and meeting varying degrees of resistance. There was often a good deal of confusion, and local independence was frequently asserted at first. The soviets, by then almost everywhere under Bolshevik control, played a crucial role, providing an organizational base and both masking and legitimizing the transfer of power. The steady march of the October Revolution across Russia was completed by the end of December, with some notable exceptions. In Tiflis, the capital of the province of Georgia in the Caucasus, local Mensheviks, a well-organized, vigorous, nationalistic group, retained control. Anti-Bolshevik forces also triumphed in the homeland of the Don and Kuban Cossacks in southeastern Russia. These were later to form the nucleus of the White armies that battled the Bolsheviks in the Russian civil war from 1918 to 1921. Finally, in the Ukraine the local government, the Rada, which had been at loggerheads with the Provisional government throughout the summer, beat back a Bolshevik challenge and set up an independent authority. But what is remarkable is the relative ease with which the Bolsheviks, despite these setbacks, were able in a few weeks to establish control over most of such a huge and diverse country.

THE MILITARY THREAT

In the beginning the Bolsheviks faced two threats from the army. The most serious was to Petrograd itself, a brief flurry stirred up by Kerensky. When the deposed prime minister reached the headquarters of the Northern Front armies at Pskov on the evening of November 7, he met a rather mixed reception. The commander was not particularly interested in helping him and in any case pointed out, quite correctly, that he had few troops who could be counted on actively to support the government. Soon, however, Kerensky got in touch with General Petr Krasnov, commander of some Cossack units, who agreed to lead an effort to recapture Petrograd. By the night of November 9–10 a small force under

PETROGRAD AT THE TIME
OF THE OCTOBER REVOLUTION

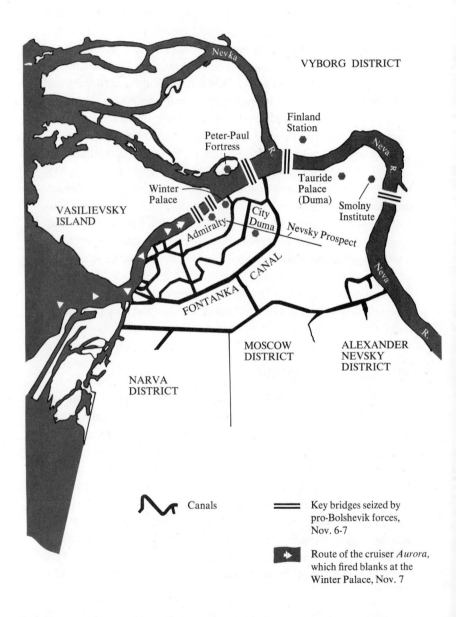

Krasnov, accompanied by Kerensky, had settled in Gatchina, about twenty-five miles south of Petrograd, to await reinforcements—which never came—and to ready an assault on the capital. Within Petrograd those opposed to the Bolsheviks rallied around the Committee for the Salvation of the Country and the Revolution, which had been formed on November 8 by moderate socialists and liberal members of the City Duma. It rejected the Bolsheviks' claim to authority, creating some difficulties by persuading many civil servants not to cooperate with the new Bolshevik rulers. Bureaucrats in a number of government departments stayed home or refused to carry out orders and would not turn over records and funds. The leaders of the committee had hoped to assist Krasnov by staging a rising against the Bolsheviks during his attack, but faulty coordination and the capture of a courier carrying their plans forced them to throw their meager forces into action prematurely on November 11. After capturing a few strategic places they were quickly overwhelmed by units of the Military Revolutionary Committee.

The following day, November 12, General Krasnov advanced on Petrograd and a lengthy, bloody, and militarily indecisive battle took place about twelve miles from the city. Unable to score a victory, Krasnov's small force of some 1,000 troops became increasingly demoralized and finally fell back on their base, where two days later they agreed to give up their struggle against the revolution and surrender Kerensky. Forewarned, Kerensky escaped in disguise and later went into exile, first in England and then in the United States, where well into the 1960s he continued to lecture audiences on the devious ways in which both the right and the left had betrayed him in 1917.

The second immediate military menace to the Bolsheviks came from Mogilev, the location of the general staff and the headquarters of the army supreme commander, General N. N. Dukhonin. The latter refused to recognize the new Bolshevik government and ordered units to mobilize against Petrograd. Because the Northern Front command was reluctant to cooperate and because detachments from the other fronts either would not go or were

intercepted by Bolshevik agitators and sympathetic railway workers, no troops actually moved on the capital except for those under
Krasnov. Although by November 14 General Dukhonin had given
up his effort to suppress the new revolutionary government, he still
spurned cooperation with it. Soon a number of anti-Bolshevik
politicians began to arrive at army headquarters with the hope of
organizing a campaign of resistance to the Soviet government.

After ignoring Lenin's instructions that he cease hostilities and
enter armistice negotiations with the Germans, Dukhonin found
himself dismissed on November 22, with instructions to await the
arrival of his replacement. It was a ticklish situation. The majority
of the soldiers were unwilling to fight either Germans or Bolsheviks, but the new Soviet government had little real control over
them. Dukhonin had the support of some loyal units near headquarters as well as many officers throughout the army. The Soviet
delegation, headed by the former sailor Nikolai Krylenko, Dukhonin's designated successor, proceeded slowly toward Mogilev,
attempting to consolidate support in the army as it went. Instead
of acting vigorously to rally anti-Bolshevik forces, Dukhonin
waited resignedly at headquarters. As the days passed, his supporters melted away, and he quietly submitted to arrest on
December 3. Although Krylenko tried to prevent it, an angry mob
of soldiers and sailors seized Dukhonin and beat him to death.
For the moment the danger of a military counterrevolution was
past, but Dukhonin's murder foreshadowed the cruel and bitter
civil war that was to break out a few months later.

THE POLITICAL CRISIS

With the capture of Moscow and the overcoming of the threats
from Krasnov and Dukhonin, the Bolsheviks had successfully met
the main military challenges to their new regime. In that same
period, however, they had to face a serious political crisis. On
November 8, when the Congress of Soviets had approved the new
cabinet (renamed the Council of People's Commissars since the
term "ministers" seemed too bourgeois and old-fashioned), the
Left SRs had refused to participate in it, though they continued

to endorse the Bolshevik takeover. Thus it was an all-Bolshevik government, which displeased many people, including moderate Bolsheviks, trade unionists, and other supporters of the October Revolution. The most important opponent of the one-party cabinet was the All-Russian Executive Committee of the Union of Railway Workers, *Vikzhel* as it was known by its initials in Russian. Since this group had the power to disrupt communications and transport systems throughout the country, Lenin could hardly ignore its demand for a coalition government of various socialist parties. Exerting maximum pressure, *Vikzhel* leaders threatened a general strike unless negotiations toward that end were opened.

The Bolsheviks had little choice but to acquiesce and talks among representatives of all the socialist parties opened on the evening of November 11. At first the moderate socialists took a tough line, still hoping that the fighting in Moscow and outside Petrograd might unseat the Bolsheviks. The latter, represented in the beginning by moderate leaders (Lenin and Trotsky were busy elsewhere), adopted a conciliatory stance. But as the talks dragged on the situation of the new government steadily improved and Lenin, now directing the negotiations, enforced an uncompromising position. Despite a serious intraparty squabble over the issue that precipitated the resignation from the Bolsheviks' Central Committee of five of its moderate members, Lenin's determination carried the day once again. After several weeks of fruitless negotiations, and when it was clear that the Bolsheviks were firmly in power, the effort to create a compromise government was abandoned. At this juncture the Left SRs agreed to accept several posts in the Soviet government, and the Central Committee members who had resigned were reappointed. The political crisis, too, was over.

THE NATURE OF THE REVOLUTION

The Bolsheviks had now not only taken power but seemed able to hold it, at least for the moment. The October Revolution was completed. But what did it mean? What sort of revolution was this?

Partly planned, partly accidental, partly the reflection of mass aspirations, the October Revolution in Russia was clearly not the classical proletarian revolution envisaged by Karl Marx. In Russia a working-class majority did not take over an advanced and productive industrial economic system, using it to provide both material well-being for all and spiritual liberation for each. Instead the Bolsheviks, a minority party, had come to power in a huge, backward agricultural country, disorganized and devastated by a great war in which it was still formally involved. Survival and a sense of direction were the most Lenin could offer.

Nor was the October Revolution like the February Revolution, a spontaneous, mass, liberationist affair. In fact, the masses were hardly evident in the October Revolution, though they undoubtedly supported its goals. It depended rather on a few leaders and a determined group of disgruntled soldiers, sailors, and workers. Its thrust was order and security, not freedom and self-indulgence.

Finally, it was not the kind of revolution Lenin and the Bolsheviks would have most desired. It had to be cloaked in the mantle of the democratic popularity of the soviets of workers' and soldiers' (and later peasants') deputies; it involved cooperation with a wavering and unreliable ally, the Left SRs; and it hinged on neutralizing the vast peasant majority of Russia by confirming their distinctly unsocialist and un-Leninist division of the land into small peasant-controlled plots.

In retrospect, the October Revolution represented the interweaving of four major strands of Russian development—two originating far back in Russian history, two springing from the events of 1917—all four being turned skillfully by the Bolsheviks to their advantage. An important key to understanding both the February and October revolutions lies in the attitudes, emotions, and psychology of the Russian lower classes. Fueled by centuries of mistreatment, oppression, and injustice, their resentment of the privileged—whether landlord, property owner, or educated professional—grew from its mild unleashing in the February Revolution into a savage, angry force that swept aside the liberals, moderate socialists, and "do-gooders" in November and turned into a cruel and burning hatred during the civil war that followed. A corollary of this deep-seated rancor against the upper classes and the bitter determination to right matters was a long-standing suspicion of foreign ideas, interests, and people.

In 1917 all of this led to misunderstanding or skepticism about Western liberal aims and practices, to rejection of any authority, and to a lack of restraint which seriously undermined the Provisional government and on which the Bolsheviks could easily capitalize (although continuation of some of these attitudes soon forced them to resort to increasing discipline and coercion). The Bolsheviks, eager to right ancient wrongs, could attack not only Russian landlords, bourgeoisie, and war profiteers but foreign imperialists and warmongers. In this way the Bolsheviks managed effectively to channel popular animus and widespread xenophobia against the government and in their favor.

Second, as we saw in Chapter Three, the February Revolution suddenly loosed urges toward gratification of individual and group desires. In some sense the year 1917 was a desperate scramble for everyone to get out of the revolution what each person most wanted. While these concerns sometimes overlapped among individuals and groups and in other cases were conflicting, they did boil down to a few basic demands. And it was the Bolsheviks who uniquely stood for—and responded to—these aspirations. The Bolshevik program struck a powerful note of concordance with popular wishes: Peace! Land! Workers' Control! Self-determination of Nationalities! No other group in Russia was as clear, and certainly no other program corresponded so closely with what a huge majority of the Russian people most desperately wanted.

Third, 1917 was marked by a spirit of genuine idealism, a naïve faith in "the revolution," among a broad spectrum of the population. Both groups and individuals fervently believed that somehow "the revolution" would improve their lot and solve their problems. The mystique of this ideal was a powerful force in 1917, and though each interpreted the meaning of the revolution differently, all clung to it as to life itself. The Bolsheviks were able to turn this to great tactical advantage. From the time of the Kornilov affair on, the Bolsheviks could use the bogey of counter-revolution to rally the masses to their side and to weaken their socialist opponents' will to resist. As the moment of insurrection approached, the Bolsheviks insisted that they were protecting the Petrograd Soviet and defending the revolution, not moving to take power. In fact, as accounts of the time make clear, many people in Russia did not see the October Revolution as a Bolshevik action at all but simply as the Soviet's defending itself against the counter-revolutionary designs of Kerensky and his cohorts.

Finally, as the historian John Keep has demonstrated, one of the surprising phenomena of 1917 was the rapid and usually spontaneous development of mass organizations—peasant land committees, soviets, soldiers' committees, factory committees, unions.[1] These proved to be highly effective instruments for mobilizing the masses and channeling their basic drives into social and political action. During the year these local organizations became increasingly centralized internally and at the same time fell under the control of regional or national units in a rapidly growing hierarchical system. Executive committees, often dominated by representatives of political parties, exerted more and more authority. Of all the groups contending in 1917 Russia, the Bolsheviks were the most skillful at infiltrating and gaining control of the mass organizations, particularly the factory committees, soldiers' committees, and soviets in towns and cities. Domination of the Petrograd and Moscow soviets was crucial to the success of the October Revolution in Russia's two major cities, and this pattern was repeated in thousands of places throughout the country and in the army. Through the mass organizations, the Bolsheviks were able to speak as if for the bulk of the population, though by the fall of 1917 the masses themselves were largely passive and politically apathetic. Later the Bolsheviks succeeded in transforming these organizations into instruments for directing and controlling the population to achieve goals set by the party.

THE THEORETICAL BASIS

Was Lenin above all an opportunist, as his detractors often claim? In a sense he certainly was. His political intuition told him

[1] John Keep, *The Russian Revolution: A Study in Mass Mobilization* (New York, 1976).

that Russia was ripe for a popular revolution and he made sure that he and his party took advantage of that opportunity. Yet Lenin was an idealist and a theorist as well, and this side of him must also be constantly borne in mind. His philosophy and goals guided and shaped much of what he did. He was a dedicated Marxist as well as a determined revolutionary, and he went to great lengths to see the events of 1917 in Russia within the framework of his ideology.

The explanation Lenin finally worked out was that two special sets of circumstances permitted the Bolsheviks to come to power and to launch a socialist revolution in Russia. First, the imperialist World War weakened world capitalism and helped produce a revolutionary situation. The imperialist system could then be breached at its most vulnerable point, Russia—the weakest link in the chain of imperialism. Moreover, when revolution broke out in Russia, the great powers were locked in such a death struggle that they were unable to direct their attention and energy against this potentially destructive attack on the flank of the system. The war shielded the revolution in Russia, permitting, Lenin hoped, the spark kindled there to burn long enough to ignite proletarian revolutions in the more advanced capitalist countries of Western Europe.

Second, Lenin believed that the workers could come to power in Russia because of the unique conditions of that country at that time. Not only the war among the imperialists but the geographical characteristics of Russia protected the fledgling revolution. The country was located on the edge of Europe, and it encompassed vast distances; it was not easy for the capitalist countries to direct forces against the upstart but potentially dangerous Soviet government. In addition, as we saw in Chapter Three, Lenin considered the proletariat in Russia relatively strong because it was highly concentrated and because the Russian bourgeoisie was relatively weak. Finally, the burning land hunger of the peasants and the general discontent created by the burdens of a senseless war produced in Russia a revolutionary situation that the Bolsheviks could take advantage of.

But even if a good Marxist accepted all this, what of the necessary progression through the stages of history? What happened to capitalism, through which semifeudal Russia must inevitably pass before reaching socialism? Here Trotsky gave Lenin a significant assist. Without delving too deeply into revolutionary ideology, we can simply summarize that beginning in 1905 Trotsky had developed the idea of uninterrupted (sometimes called "permanent") revolution. It was a theory nicely suited to the Russian situation. It held that once a capitalist revolution occurred, the workers under determined leadership might continue to push in a radical direction until that revolution was transformed into a socialist revolution, which would then spread from Russia into Western Europe. Thus the revolution proceeded, without a break, from the capitalist or bourgeois-democratic phase into a socialist revolution and from backward Russia into advanced Europe. In 1917 Lenin borrowed this basic idea, adding that the poorest peasantry would support the workers and help them push the revolution forward. He concluded that by seizing power the proletariat and peasantry could fulfill the capitalist stage "in passing."

Exactly how this was to come about was left vague, but Lenin was consistent with Marxism by going on to say that of course the Russian revolutionaries could only *begin* a socialist revolution. Because Russia did not possess the advanced industry necessary for socialism, the Russian Revolution could be *completed* only with the aid of socialist revolutions in Western Europe. Once the workers seized power there, they could use the European countries' advanced productive forces to channel aid to the Russian proletariat and to help them complete the socialist revolution in Russia. Despite Joseph Stalin's later misinterpretation of Lenin in the debates of the 1920s between Stalin and Trotsky, Lenin never believed—right up to his death in 1924—that socialism could be achieved in Russia alone, without help from the advanced countries.

This theoretical belief had a number of implications for Lenin's actions and Soviet policy. It meant, for example, that at first Lenin saw the October Revolution as only the beginning, as a toehold for the international socialist revolution. Consequently, he developed his concept of the Russian revolutionaries' "holding on" to power until aid from the West reached them. The sense of the following quotation was repeated many times by Lenin between 1918 and 1921:

> We do not lose sight of the weakness of the Russian working class as compared with other detachments of the international proletariat. . . . But we must remain at our post until our ally, the international proletariat, comes to our aid. . . . Although we see that this proletariat is moving too slowly, owing to objective circumstances, we must nevertheless stick to our tactics of waiting and taking advantage of the conflicts and antagonisms among the imperialists, and of slowly accumulating strength—the tactics of maintaining the island of Soviet power intact amidst the raging sea of imperialism, of maintaining intact that island to which the eyes of the working people of all countries are even now turned.[2]

Two things followed from this conviction of Lenin's. In the first place, it was vitally important that everything possible be done—including all sorts of compromises in domestic policy and concessions to external enemies—for the Soviet government to retain power, thereby protecting the flame of revolution in Russia, which would later help spark revolution in Europe. Second, when no proletarian revolutions occurred in the West, Lenin realized reluctantly that he would have to start trying to build socialism in Russia. In my opinion, however, he was quite uncertain how to proceed and he still felt that he could not fully succeed without help from outside. He died in 1924 without resolving this issue in his own mind.

STAYING IN POWER

In the fall of 1917, working from these premises, Lenin therefore had one overriding concern—to cling to power at whatever

[2] V. I. Lenin, *Sochineniia,* 2nd ed. (30 vols., Moscow, 1928–1929), XXIII, p. 16.

cost. This meant giving in to popular pressure where to deny it would jeopardize the Bolsheviks' rule, and deflecting or rejecting mass demands where to yield would mean a diminution or loss of the Bolsheviks' power. The first issue, and one that was to plague Lenin and the Bolsheviks for some months, was the war. On this matter they had little choice. The one party that had consistently opposed the war, at least since April, the Bolsheviks had been borne into power partly by the mass surge of revulsion against the wasting and losing military struggle. The Bolsheviks had promised peace and if they didn't deliver, the masses would soon turn against them.

Consequently, it is no surprise that the first business Lenin put before the Second All-Russian Congress of Soviets on the evening of November 8 was adoption of the decree on peace he had drafted earlier that day. It read in part: "The Workers' and Peasants' Government . . . proposes to all combatant peoples and their governments to begin immediate negotiations for an honest democratic peace . . . an immediate peace without annexations (i.e., without the seizure of foreign land, without the forcible taking over of foreign nationalities) and without contributions [reparations]." The decree went on to call for annulling the secret treaties tsarist Russia had concluded. Lenin proposed a three-month armistice and ended by appealing especially to the workers of England, France, and Germany to help achieve peace.

Whether Lenin seriously expected this rather bombastic proclamation to lead to peace is uncertain. On a number of occasions in this period and during the following couple of years he seems genuinely to have overestimated the revolutionary ardor of the European proletariat, and perhaps he indeed hoped that the Russion example might touch off popular indignation and disorders that would force the German and Allied governments to end the hostilities. It seems more likely, however, that the decree was intended primarily as a message of reassurance to the Russian people and a propagandistic call to Europeans, with the realization that it was unlikely to produce immediate and concrete results. In fact it didn't. Most Russians were pleased, but the warring governments ignored Lenin's appeal and it stirred hardly a ripple in the tranquil pond of patriotic support of the war by the European masses.

Lenin's position did, however, have one significant and unintended effect. In the following weeks the attractiveness of his peace program led the British and American governments to review their announced war aims and spurred President Woodrow Wilson to present, in January 1918, his famous Fourteen Points, which later became the liberal platform for the Versailles peace negotiations and a bone of contention between Wilson and the Allied leaders.

All the European governments treated the new Soviet government gingerly, without of course granting it official recognition. Not only did they think it couldn't last, but they were puzzled as well as shocked by its radical program and unorthodox behavior. But because the Allies wanted to avoid doing anything that might encourage or force the Russians to withdraw from the war, and because the Germans were anxious not to obstruct the Bolsheviks' avowed intention to stop fighting, both sides were extremely cautious in their initial informal relations with the Soviet government. No one, however, was prepared to accept Lenin's offer to enter general peace negotiations since each side hoped to win the war in 1918. After a few weeks, the Germans, anxious to get the Russians out of the war before spring (which would release German troops for a major offensive on the Western Front planned for the spring of 1918), prepared to advance farther into Russia. Since the Russian army was totally demoralized and virtually leaderless, there was nothing to stop them.

In this situation Lenin, as we saw earlier, ordered the army to open negotiations for an immediate cease-fire on the Russian fronts alone, and in December, after General Dukhonin had been replaced, an armistice was signed with Germany and Austria-Hungary. Most Russians were delighted that the fighting had stopped, but some saw it as a "sellout" of the country to the German militarists and a betrayal of the Allies. During the winter, as negotiations for peace with Germany dragged on and it became clear that the Germans were demanding a draconian settlement, a major debate broke out in the country as a whole and within the Bolshevik party itself over what to do. Patriots wanted to resume the battle, but there was no army to do so. Many Bolsheviks favored a policy of "revolutionary war"—attempting to carry the struggle to the Germans, to subvert the enemy soldiers, and to spark a proletarian revolution in the German and Austrian empires. This was also quite unrealistic, as the German generals proved by continuing their advance into Russia following a breakdown in the negotiations. A group led by Trotsky propounded a formula of "no war, no peace" but in practice this solved nothing and failed to stop the Germans.

At last, Lenin, once more with fierce determination and after one defeat and a long fight in the party's top committees, managed to push through his own policy, which was to make peace with the Germans at whatever price. Lenin argued, quite correctly as events turned out, that a clear-cut peace settlement was needed to prevent the Germans from occupying most of Russia, to retain popular support for the Soviet government, and to permit reconstruction in the country and restoration of the economy. He insisted that it was the only way to "hold on," to save the revolution. The concessions forced upon the Soviet government would be temporary, he said, to be overturned when the Germans were defeated and the European proletarian revolution broke out. So in March 1918 the Soviet government signed the Treaty of Brest-Litovsk, under which Russia lost a quarter of its territory and population and a third of its industry. For the moment the revolution was rescued and the Bolsheviks retained power.

In the longer term, however, Lenin's policy led to major difficulties for the Bolsheviks. Their allies, the Left SRs, and many nationalistically minded Russians who were otherwise sympathetic to the Soviet government felt that the country had been betrayed and bitterly opposed the Brest-Litovsk peace. In a matter of weeks this opposition led to the SRs' breaking with the Bolsheviks, and it helped precipitate the full-scale struggle between "Reds" and "Whites" that erupted in the summer of 1918. The Brest peace also contributed to the initial decision of the Allies and the United States to intervene by force in Russia in order to try to reopen an Eastern Front against the Germans. Thus Lenin's peace policy was a factor in bringing on almost three more years of civil war and foreign intervention in Russia. Yet the alternative might well have been German occupation and the demise of the Soviet government.

Lenin's second act on coming to power also conformed to popular demands. On November 8, after the Congress of Soviets had approved the decree on peace, he presented for its endorsement a decree on land. Quite at variance with Bolshevik ideology, it confirmed the division of land by the peasants that had steadily taken place since midsummer. Some observers have seen the decree as another example of Lenin's political sensitivity and skill and have described it as a master stroke that neutralized the peasantry. In fact Lenin had no choice. The Bolsheviks had promised the land to the peasants. The latter, by acting on that promise, had helped to undermine the Provisional government, and they would have rejected the new Soviet government if it had done anything else but endorse their seizure of the land. At that juncture there was no force in Russia strong enough to reverse, or even to modify significantly, what the peasants had done.

From the standpoint of ideological purists, Lenin's land decree not only rejected earlier Bolshevik theory on this issue but, worst of all, it also drew unabashedly from the SR program. Both Lenin and the peasants agreed in 1917 that private land should be confiscated without compensation to the owners, but the Bolsheviks believed that its ownership should be vested in the state and that large estates should not be broken up but retained as socialist units of agricultural production to provide models for the peasantry. The Bolsheviks wanted to put village communes under state control and to mechanize and socialize agricultural production. The peasants, on the other hand, wanted an egalitarian distribution of the land among those who worked it.

Recognizing the strength of peasant feelings but anxious to preserve the state's interest, Lenin made his decree on land fuzzy on the question of ownership. The land was transferred to the peasants pending action by the Constituent Assembly, but the decree acknowledged the right of peasants and communes to use it as if it were theirs. This last was what the Socialist Revolutionaries had urged, and when a few members of the Congress of Soviets reminded Lenin of this he replied simply, "As a democratic government we cannot disregard the decision of the masses, even if we disagree with it. . . . Life itself is the best teacher, and it will show who is right; let the peasants solve this question from one end and we from the other."[3] As it turned out, Lenin's decree, while politically necessary, solved nothing from the standpoint of the Soviet government. After intermittent skirmishes between the new regime and the peasants until 1921, and a truce from 1921 to 1928, Stalin's great collectivization drive of the late 1920s and early 1930s touched off a full-scale war over who was to control the land. Millions of lives were lost and agricultural production declined sharply.

On a number of other important issues Lenin and the Bolsheviks attempted to deflect revolutionary currents in directions that would ensure the party's retaining power. For example, the importance of the factory committees and of the slogan "Workers' Control" in bringing the Bolsheviks to power meant that the idea of worker participation in running industry could not be repudiated at once. On the other hand, the economy was in chaos and many factories could not operate at all because of lack of discipline or because fuel and raw materials were not available. To try to maintain or restore production required centralized control and authority, not groups of workers puzzling over how to manage complex production units. Thus, while acknowledging the principle of workers' control, the Bolsheviks set about capturing and manipulating the factory committees and trade unions, and in December 1917 they set up the Supreme Council of the National Economy, which tried to operate the Russian economy as a system of centralized state capitalism. The proletarian "controllers" were eased out before long, and bureaucrats have run Soviet industry ever since.

[3] Quoted in William Henry Chamberlin, *The Russian Revolution, 1917–1921* (2 vols., New York, 1935; reprinted 1965), I, p. 326.

In a similar way the new leaders of Russia made obeisance to the masses' wish that private ownership of economic resources be abolished and all economic property be transferred to the people while carrying this out only where it would not interfere with their effort to revive the economy. Thus the banks were nationalized and put under state control and all former state bonds and obligations were annulled. But private industry was left in the hands of its former owners on the grounds that seizing it would only further disrupt production. Only many months later, in the early summer of 1918, was most industry nationalized and taken over by the government.

In the political arena, we saw earlier in the chapter how Lenin skillfully diverted the popular aspiration for a coalition government of all the socialist parties by first dragging out the negotiations with *Vikzhel* and then co-opting the Left Socialist Revolutionaries as minor partners in the government. On another important issue, the fate of the non-Russian minorities, the Bolsheviks also seemed to yield to revolutionary demands while in fact harnessing them to their own determination to stay in power. During 1917 the Bolsheviks had gained much sympathy among the peoples on the borderlands of the empire by espousing the slogan of self-determination for all national groups. When Stalin became People's Commissar of Nationalities in the new government, this slogan was reaffirmed. But in practice, particularly in the treatment of groups in the Caucasus and of the Ukrainians, it became clear that people had the right to determine their own future as long as that future fitted in with the plans and needs of the Bolshevik party and the Soviet government. And so it remains to this day.

In one key area, however, the Bolsheviks defiantly rejected a major popular demand of the summer and got away with it. All parties, including the Bolsheviks, had had as a major goal convocation of the Constituent Assembly as soon as possible. This unanimity reflected the hold in people's minds of the idea of being able for the first time in their lives to control their own destinies. When the Bolsheviks came to power the scheduled date for Constituent Assembly elections was only a few weeks away. Though

Lenin would clearly have preferred to cancel them, it was finally decided not to risk popular indignation and the elections were held, with remarkably little interference except for some harassment of the Kadet party's campaign. The results of the only general democratic election in Russian history were revealing—and about as the Bolsheviks had expected:

Parties	Votes (millions)	% of Vote	Assembly Seats
SRs	20.9	58%	410
Bolsheviks	9	25%	175
Kadets, etc.	4.6	13%	103
Mensheviks	1.7	4%	16

Since the bulk of the voters were peasants, the strong showing of the SRs was not surprising. As long as the decree on land had won the support or neutrality of the rural population for the new government, what political party the peasants voted for made little effective difference in the Bolsheviks' ability to hold power. Moreover, the Bolsheviks had won in a number of major cities, including Moscow and Petrograd, and had finished a close second to the SRs in the army. Consequently, the election results were more of a nuisance than a threat to the Bolsheviks.

After a brief but lively dispute among the party leaders, the Bolsheviks decided to permit the Constituent Assembly to meet but to dissolve it if it failed to endorse a Bolshevik program prepared for it. On January 18 the assembly convened, and as expected the Bolsheviks, even with some Left SR support, were in a minority. After hours of debate, which included courageous denunciations of the growing Bolshevik dictatorship and a refusal to endorse the Bolshevik program, the session was adjourned when the guards provided for the Constituent Assembly by the Soviet government told the chairman that they were tired and wanted to go home. The next day the Soviet government ordered the assembly's dissolution, and when the deputies returned to the hall armed soldiers turned them away. The closing of the Constituent Assembly stirred almost no public protest or outcry.

Although it seems surprising at first that an institution so unanimously endorsed over the summer could so easily be disbanded, the situation had changed considerably by January 1918. Except for a few politicians and intellectuals, most people had lost interest in the ideals the Constituent Assembly represented. They were more concerned with daily survival under the new regime, the prospects for peace with the Germans, demobilization, allocating the seized land, and getting enough food and fuel to last through the winter. Many people were politically numb or apathetic; others were afraid; and still others, benefiting from some of the Soviet government's initial measures, were unwilling to oppose the new leaders just yet. In short, only a handful of Russians were prepared in the wintry days of January 1918 to risk their lives to defend this abstract symbol of representative government and popular sovereignty that had seemed to mean so much only a few months earlier. Those who were soon drifted off to the embryonic centers of anti-Bolshevik resistance, and in one case—in Siberia—they helped form one of the coalitions that engaged the Bolsheviks in civil war in 1918.

With the dispersal of the Constituent Assembly in January and the acceptance of the Brest-Litovsk peace in early March 1918, the Bolsheviks had succeeded in consolidating their grip on power and in carrying out the main lines of their initial program. To be sure, they faced complicated and formidable challenges in food and agricultural policy and in reconstructing and reviving the shattered economy of Russia, and they were soon forced to defend themselves against widespread counterrevolutionary movements and scattered foreign intervention. But for the moment they were secure. The unlikely revolution had been made and won.

9
Fulfillment or Betrayal?

★

We need now to consider the meaning of the Russian Revolution. The way in which the Bolsheviks came to power in the October Revolution and their early efforts to retain power contributed significantly to several major features that have characterized the Soviet state and society ever since: centralization of power and lack of popular participation in decision making; party domination of the soviets and the soviets' lack of any important independent authority; and a one-party dictatorship in the political life of the country.

To begin with the soviets, there is little doubt that from the late summer of 1917 through the end of the year the soviets represented the will of the majority of politically concerned Russians and accurately reflected popular wishes and aspirations. What most delegates in the soviets wanted was a new government responsive to the system of soviets, both to the national congress and to the local units. Yet the fate of the soviets was foreshadowed when Lenin finally convinced other party leaders not to let the Second All-Russian Congress of Soviets direct the transfer of power or determine the composition of the new government but to present it with a *fait accompli*. According to the British historian John

Keep, the Bolsheviks, as they increasingly gained majorities in city, district, regional, and provincial soviets from August on, managed many of these bodies in such a way as both to assist and to mask the Bolshevik bid for power.[1] Moreover, once in power, the Bolsheviks never turned the soviets back to the people. They kept the form but the party controlled the substance. Still today the soviets symbolize popular participation in government while in fact serving primarily as "transmission belts" for channeling the directives of the party to the people.

At the same time that the Bolsheviks were beginning to dominate and subordinate the soviets, the party took the first step toward setting up its dictatorship in the country. Most delegates to the Second Congress of Soviets wanted a revolutionary government that would include the other socialist parties and that would represent the broadest range of anti-Kerensky and anticapitalist forces. Nevertheless, the Bolsheviks established a one-party government because Lenin and most of his closest advisers were determined not to share power. Almost forced by the pressure of *Vikzhel* to accept a coalition government with the other socialist parties, Lenin stalled and then drew in the Left SRs as a gesture. In dissolving the Constituent Assembly, Lenin and the Bolsheviks simply set the seal on a policy they had already formulated—that they would establish a one-party dictatorship and brook no political opposition. Although at times during the civil war Menshevik and other non-Bolshevik papers were allowed to publish briefly, and although other parties were not entirely suppressed until 1922, there was never any doubt, from 1917 on, that Soviet rule meant Bolshevik rule.

As a logical outgrowth of these decisions, it was not long before the Bolsheviks resorted to coercion to maintain their one-party dictatorship. In December 1917 the Extraordinary Commission to Combat Counterrevolution and Sabotage was formed, known by its Russian initials as the *Cheka*. In the beginning it was a small organization and hunted criminals and bandits as much as political

---

[1] John Keep, *The Russian Revolution: A Study in Mass Mobilization* (New York, 1976).

enemies. Before long, however, it had begun to earn its later worldwide notoriety as an instrument of political terror and repression.

To some degree the party's domination of the soviets and the establishment of a one-party dictatorship over the country resulted from beliefs and attitudes that Lenin and the top Bolshevik leaders had developed over the previous fifteen years of struggle against both the tsarist government and liberal groups and other revolutionaries. Yet the events of 1917—the Bolsheviks' class war against the Kadets and the bourgeoisie, their repudiation of the socialists in the Provisional government, and their efforts in the June demonstration, the July Days, and the Kornilov affair to stay close to but not to be led or pushed by the masses—intensified the Leninists' distrust of mass organizations and other parties. The course of the revolution reinforced their belief that they knew what was best for the people and that their way was the correct way. Finally, it hardened their determination not to share power. To be sure, as Alexander Rabinowitch has shown, there was still a good deal of openness within the party (the dictatorship within the party evolved later) and the party did try to respond to popular aspirations,[2] but the fact remains that the Bolshevik leaders had no intention of letting the people decide important issues such as the form and composition of the new Soviet government or whether to make a separate peace with the Germans. Moreover, since the masses had not really participated in the October Revolution, there was little reason for the Bolsheviks to be beholden to them. The revolution had been the culmination of a great revolutionary surge, but a relatively small group had engineered the actual transfer of power. Looking back, we can see that there never was much chance of popular participation in the new Soviet government, given the level of political consciousness in Russia, the traditions of the country, and the fundamental attitude of the Bolsheviks.

On the other hand, alongside the rather grim effects of 1917 discussed above were more promising outcomes of the Russian

[2] Alexander Rabinowitch, *The Bolsheviks Come to Power: The Revolution of 1917 in Petrograd* (New York, 1976).

Revolution. If the Bolsheviks betrayed one set of revolutionary aspirations—those connected with justice, civil freedom, and popular participation in government—they fulfilled another. In many ways the Bolsheviks directly reflected popular desires and needs, and they acted rapidly to give the peasants land, to bring peace, to temper economic exploitation, and to give many people a sense of dignity and self-worth that they had never had before. That most of these things didn't last, that the Soviet regime turned into a cruel and abhorrent system of terror under Stalin, is another story, beyond the scope of this brief account. Still, by the end of 1917, a judicious observer would have had to say that the Bolshevik balance sheet, measured by what happened to individuals and groups, was at best mixed. The people had gained and they had lost, as so often happens at major turning points in human history.

CIVIL WAR AND FOREIGN INTERVENTION

In the next few years events in Russia were more terrible and confused, but in many ways less complicated and important, than those of 1917. In the first months after the October Revolution the most important issue was how to end the war with Germany and Austria-Hungary. Once the Treaty of Brest-Litovsk had been signed in March 1918, incipient divisions within the country soon erupted into civil war and foreign intervention.

Many who opposed the Bolsheviks were patriotically motivated, believing that the country and the revolution had been betrayed to the Germans. In addition, there was a broad spectrum of opponents, from moderate socialists (and even anarchists) to monarchists, who rejected various social, economic, cultural, and political policies of the Bolsheviks. Finally, national minorities in the Baltic, the Ukraine, the Caucasus, and Central Asia fought for autonomy or independence. Thus the anti-Bolsheviks, or Whites, were a motley collection with often disparate and even conflicting purposes. For example, conservative White leaders such as General A. I. Denikin, favoring a unified, centralized Russia, strongly opposed the nationalities' strivings for greater independence.

This internecine struggle was complicated by the decision of the Allied powers, together with a reluctant United States, to intervene in Russia. The primary reasons were at first anti-German: the Allies wanted to save war supplies stored in Russia from falling into German hands and they hoped to support groups in Russia, either Red or White, who would be willing to continue the war against Germany. After initial hesitation, the Soviet government opposed the Allied intervention and soon Allied aid and troops were arriving in North Russia and Siberia in support of White forces, and the intervention took on a strongly anti-Bolshevik cast.

Encircled by foreign and domestic attackers, the Bolsheviks waged an uphill fight, hanging on to power only in the central part of the country for the next two and a half years. They imposed centralized control over economic and political life and enforced it with terror, as needed. Drawing on Trotsky's brilliant leadership and administrative skill, they built a well-trained, dedicated, and substantial Red Army to fight counterrevolutionary Whites and foreign interventionists. They pursued a vacillating policy toward the peasants, requisitioning grain by force but leaving them the divided land.

The Allied defeat of Germany and Austria-Hungary in November 1918 led neither to revolution in Europe as Lenin had hoped (despite a few minor outbreaks), nor to the end of foreign intervention in Russia. President Wilson would have preferred to withdraw from Russia, but his partners wanted to stamp out what they perceived as a revolutionary disease that might spread to Western Europe. The last American troops came home in January 1920, but the British, French, and Japanese continued to assist the Whites, primarily with money and munitions. On the other hand, war-weariness and sympathy for the Reds on the part of some workers in the West made it impossible for the Western powers to intervene fully, and they were unable to send an expeditionary force into Russia to crush the Bolsheviks as Marshal Foch of France and Winston Churchill of England would have liked to do.

Moreover, the Whites were not as formidable enemies as they might have been. They were disunited and largely pursued reactionary policies that antagonized the populations in the regions they controlled. Too chauvinistic and shortsighted to recognize the rights of minority groups, the Whites lost the cooperation of those non-Russians who opposed the Bolsheviks, which might have provided the margin of added strength needed to permit the Whites to topple the Soviet regime. By the spring of 1921 the Bolsheviks had repelled the foreign interventionists, including a late entrant, the new Polish government, as well as all major White forces. Finland and the Baltic provinces of Latvia, Lithuania, and Estonia had asserted their independence, but the Bolsheviks were able to reincorporate most of the Ukraine into the Soviet state and within a year the Caucasus and the Far Eastern region as well. The Bolshevik (now renamed Communist) party and the Soviet government were solidly in control, and the revolution in Russia was finally secure. The cost in loss of life, destruction, and embitterment had been enormous, but the first "socialist" state had been launched.

THE SIGNIFICANCE OF THE RUSSIAN REVOLUTION

But was the Russian Revolution a *socialist* revolution? Those who insist that a socialist revolution must occur in an advanced industrial country in which the workers form a large majority of the population say "No." Russia in 1917 was only partly industrialized and proletarians formed only a small minority of the people. Because of this, the factories, mines, and workshops, though taken over by the state, did not belong to the workers. Instead, the government, on behalf of the people, owned the means of production, a situation characterized by some as "state capitalism." Other commentators maintain that since the Bolshevik party had to use political power to impose industrialization and socialist policies on Russia from the top down, the outcome of the revolution could at best be classified as inverted socialism or a distorted form of socialism.

Nevertheless, others contend that the Russian Revolution was

a genuine socialist revolution. They concede that Russia did not
seem a likely place for a socialist revolution but, with Lenin, they
point out that special conditions in Russia and the world provided
this golden opportunity. The uneven development of capitalism
in Russia and in the world, the death struggle among the giant
imperialist powers known as World War I, the vigor and determination of the Russian workers and their leaders, and the possibility of rallying much of the Russian peasantry to the banner of
proletarian revolution all meant that workers supported by poorer
peasants were able in Russia at that particular moment in history
to overthrow the old order, take over the land and means of production, and put into effect policies of just distribution and social
equity that would lead to socialism. The result was indeed not a
classic instance of socialist revolution (i.e., in an advanced industrial country with a proletarian majority) but a special case
which could nevertheless inspire socialist revolutions elsewhere in
the world. Moreover, despite the unfavorable circumstances of war,
counterrevolution, civil war, and foreign intervention, the Soviet
government and peoples, led by the Bolshevik party, were eventually able to build socialism in one country and to complete the
socialist revolution in Russia.

A second and related question is whether the Russian Revolution was a *democratic* socialist revolution. Soviet writers argue
vigorously that it initiated true economic and social democracy
through the policies espoused by the Bolsheviks, who simply reflected the wishes of the toiling masses, and genuine political
democracy through the governmental system of soviets, the members of which were directly elected by over 99 percent of the
voters. Others, however, believe that although the revolution had
the potential of achieving both true socialism (the collective ownership by the whole society of the basic means of production) and
democratic participation in formulating and managing the policies
of the new society, this hope was frustrated. Various explanations
are advanced of why the movement toward social democracy was
derailed: the character, prerevolutionary experience, and policies
of Lenin and his supporters; the need for strict discipline and

centralized control if the revolution was to survive war, counter-revolution, and foreign intervention; and the backward economic and social conditions of Russia, which dictated a forced rather than a voluntaristic progression toward socialism. All these critics agree that the outcome of the Russian Revolution was not democratic socialism but dictatorial socialism or totalitarian state capitalism.

Whether or not the Russian Revolution was a model to the world of a socialist or democratic socialist revolution, can it not be viewed in still another light? Was it perhaps an early example of a modernizing revolution, a pattern later emulated in such diverse countries as Turkey, China, Cuba, and Bolivia? In this interpretation the events of 1917 and after represent a dramatic and violent rejection of premodern Russian society. Only by thus breaking sharply with the values and institutions of the past could those leaders committed to the modernization of Russia mobilize the resources and establish the discipline necessary to move Russian society to a complex, highly industrialized stage. Revolutionary slogans and socialist goals were simply symbols for the basic drive to modernization and great power status in the world. The success of the Russian Revolution in initiating this process is precisely what has made it attractive to the developing countries of Asia, Africa, and Latin America (and correspondingly of much less interest to developed societies in Europe and North America). For many striving to achieve modernity the revolution represents a way of bursting the fetters of the old society and launching a struggle to achieve power and well-being.

A corollary of this theory is that not only was the Russian Revolution a breakthrough toward modernization, but its consequence was that revolutionary modernization in Russia could be achieved only at an accelerated pace and by imposing iron discipline on the whole population. This was so because Soviet Russia in the 1920s and 1930s was surrounded by powerful, expansive, already modernized, ideologically hostile neighbors in Europe and Asia. If Russia had not built strength quickly, both the state and the experiment in revolutionary socialism would have been swallowed up by stronger foreign enemies. As Stalin declared in 1930, Russia was tired of being beaten and had only ten years to overcome its backwardness. In 1941 the Navis invaded the Soviet Union.

To modernize speedily required mobilizing all the material and human resources of the country. Yet much of the population was poorly educated and not oriented toward such an effort. Therefore, if industrialization were to succeed, tight control, careful planning, and coercion (as well as incentives) were needed. Wishes and needs of individuals and groups had to be subordinated to the total and absolute direction and authority of the state and the party. As a result, the revolution led to increasing centralization and state control, culminating in a totalitarian dictatorship under Stalin after 1930.

Another corollary of the modernization thesis is that the Russian Revolution was essentially a revolt by the Bolshevik leaders and the people against the crushing encroachment of the modernized West. It represented their desperate effort to find a separate and unique path of development. In this view the revolution is seen as both an acceptance of the technical and industrial resources of the West and a vigorous attempt to preserve the special characteristics of Russian tradition and civilization. The outcome, it was hoped, might be a powerful and developed society different from and independent of the West, which could make its own particular contribution to world culture.

Quite apart from these theoretical considerations, the practical influence of the Russian Revolution on modern history is hard to overestimate. The most obvious effects stem from the role that Russia, reorganized and revitalized under Communist leadership, has played in European and world politics ever since. While it is true that with its rich resources, vast territory, and large population Russia in time would probably have been a major factor in world affairs under any sort of leadership, in 1917 the alternatives to the Bolsheviks were anarchy (and possible occupation by the Germans) or some form of military dictatorship. In either case it would have been a long time before Russia could have emerged as a power in the world. As Theodore von Laue has pointed out, the Bolsheviks succeeded in curbing anarchic tendencies in Russia and in imposing a harsh discipline.[3] This permitted effective mobilization of the country's people and resources and rapid industrialization and modernization, even under a benighted political system.

The Communists' success in modernizing Russia and in strengthening the country economically and militarily made Russia, largely shunned and ignored in the 1920s, an important factor in the 1930s, from the Spanish Civil War through the Nazi attack on the Soviet Union in 1941. Barely surviving that assault, the Soviet regime went on to play a major role in the defeat and annihilation of Hitler and the Third Reich. Emerging from World War II as the world's second most powerful country, the Soviet Union has advanced its interests worldwide, and the tension between the United States and the Soviet Union has dominated the history of the past few decades. Moreover, despite the growing rivalry of Communist China, it is apparent that the Soviet Union will continue to be the most powerful socialist country and a key actor in world politics for the remainder of this century.

More intriguing than the military and diplomatic roles of postrevolutionary Russia in world affairs, however, are the inspirational and ideological effects of the Russian Revolution. World War I dealt a major blow to the growth of international socialism; socialists had preached peace but their workers and parties patriotically supported the war efforts of their respective countries. It is ironic that Lenin, who opposed the dominant moderate trend in the worldwide socialist movement, helped save the ideology of socialism and the movement as a whole by establishing in Russia his own revolutionary brand of socialism. Through the 1920s and 1930s the existence of a socialist state in Russia stimulated opposition to capitalism and fascism and hopes for a revolution in many countries.

After World War II peasants, workers, intellectuals, and revo-

[3] Theodore H. von Laue, *Why Lenin? Why Stalin? A Reappraisal of the Russian Revolution, 1900–1930* (Philadelphia, 1964).

lutionary leaders who carried out successful Communist revolutions in China, Vietnam, and Cuba were inspired in part by the ideals of the Russian Revolution and by the existence of a socialist state in Russia. The Soviet Union provided surprisingly little direct aid to these revolutions in their initial stages, and although all of these upheavals were directed primarily against intolerable local conditions and Marxist-Leninist ideology was considerably adapted to each situation, it is still hard to imagine these major changes occurring without the example of the Russian Revolution. Thus, as part of the legacy of 1917 in Russia, a third of the world's population lives today under nominally socialist governments, and some countries in the Third World still look to the Russian model as a way to overcome backwardness, develop strength, and achieve a better life for their people. Despite the Stalinist tarnishing of this image and the competition from China, it seems probable that the goals of the Russian Revolution will continue to appeal to oppressed and downtrodden groups.

Yet in many ways the promise of the Russian Revolution remains unfulfilled. After the French Revolution it was the next great effort of people in history to grasp that elusive combination of equity, freedom, economic security, and spontaneity that seems necessary for the good life in modern society. Certainly many Russians who poured into the streets of Petrograd in March 1917 or jeered Kerensky in November fervently believed that the revolution would end injustice, protect individual choice and rights, provide a decent livelihood, and permit them to live in dignity and without fear. It didn't all work out that way, but many peoples and societies today are still striving to achieve the aspirations that inspired the Russian revolutionaries of 1917.

Guide to Further Reading

The best general account of the revolutionary period from 1917 to 1921 remains William Henry Chamberlin, *The Russian Revolution, 1917–1921** (2 vols., New York, 1965), first published in 1935. Western and Soviet books published since World War II have added new information and points of view, but Chamberlin's clear, well-written, dispassionate account is enhanced by his use of rare documents and periodicals and his interviews with key participants in the revolution.

A well-written interpretation of a broader period is Theodore H. Von Laue, *Why Lenin? Why Stalin? A Reappraisal of the Russian Revolution, 1900–1930** (Philadelphia, 1964), in which the author argues that the revolution unleashed deep-rooted anarchic tendencies in Russian society, forces which required the controlling discipline of industrialization and Stalinism. John Keep, *The Russian Revolution: A Study in Mass Mobilization* (New York, 1976) focuses on soviets, factory committees and other populist organizations, which, Keep argues, the Bolsheviks came to dominate. Petitions, telegrams, and charters from a variety of groups that reflected popular hopes and needs in the spring of 1917 are analyzed in Marc Ferro, *The Russian Revolution of February 1917,* trans. J. L. Richards (Englewood Cliffs, N. J., 1972).

* Available in paperback.

A useful general account of the background to the revolution is Lionel Kochan, *Russia in Revolution, 1890–1918* (London, 1966). A broad look at prerevolutionary Russian society based in part on first-hand observation is D. M. Wallace, *Russia on the Eve of War and Revolution* (New York, 1962). An important article arguing the likelihood that Russia was headed for revolution is Leopold Haimson, "The Problem of Social Stability in Urban Russia, 1905–1917," *Slavic Review*, 23, no. 4 (1964), 620–642, and 24, no. 1 (1965), 1–22. Several books provide detailed information on the politics of the years immediately preceding the overthrow of the tsar: Michael T. Florinsky, *The Fall of the Russian Empire** (New York, 1961); George Katkov, *Russia 1917: The February Revolution* (New York, 1967); and Sir Bernard Pares, *The Fall of the Russian Monarchy* (New York, 1961). A popular version is Robert K. Massie, *Nicholas and Alexandra** (New York, 1967), which contains good descriptions of court life and useful characterizations but overemphasizes Rasputin's role and passes over the fundamental causes of the tsardom's collapse.

Lively Marxist histories are Marcel Liebman, *The Russian Revolution,* trans. Arnold J. Pomerans (New York, 1972) and Leon Trotsky, *The History of the Russian Revolution,* trans. Max Eastman (3 vols., (London, 1967). E. H. Carr, *The Bolshevik Revolution, 1917–1923* (3 vols., New York 1951–1953) contains a lot of detail placed in an abstract Marxist framework.

In the past decade several excellent monographs by young Western scholars have treated specific aspects of the revolution, notably two by Alexander Rabinowitch: *Prelude to Revolution: The Petrograd Bolsheviks and the July Uprising* (Bloomington, Ind., 1968) and *The Bolsheviks Come to Power: The Revolution of 1917 in Petrograd** (New York, 1976). Others are Ronald G. Suny, *The Baku Commune, 1917–1918* (Princeton, N. J., 1972) and Allan K. Wildman, *The End of the Russian Imperial Army: The Old Army and the Soldiers' Revolt, March–April 1917* (Princeton, N. J., 1979). These have argued persuasively that the Bolsheviks reflected and acted in concert with deep-seated radical aspirations and actions of the masses, and the authors challenge older interpretations that the Bolsheviks came to power more or less accidentally—Robert V. Daniels, *Red October** (New York, 1967)— or in a conspiratorial *coup d'état*—Leonard Schapiro, *Origins of the Communist Autocracy* (New York, 1965).

* Available in paperback.

A definitive biography of Lenin has not yet appeared but much information about him is found in Adam B. Ulam, *The Bolsheviks** (New York, 1965). Alfred G. Meyer, *Leninism* (Cambridge, Mass., 1957) contains a clear, concise analysis of Lenin's ideology. Excellent biographies of other revolutionary leaders are: Isaac Deutscher, *The Prophet Armed: Trotsky, 1879–1921** (New York, 1954); Irving Howe, *Leon Trotsky* (New York, 1978); Robert C. Tucker, *Stalin as Revolutionary 1879–1929: A Study in History and Personality** (New York, 1973); Bertram D. Wolfe, *Three Who Made a Revolution** (Boston, 1948), which treats Lenin, Trotsky, and Stalin; Stephen F. Cohen, *Bukharin and the Russian Revolution** (New York, 1973); Israel Getzler, *Martov: A Political Biography of a Russian Social Democrat* (London, 1967); and Thomas Riha, *A Russian European: Paul Miliukov in Russian Politics* (South Bend, Ind., 1969). Alexander M. Kerensky speaks for himself in his *Russia and History's Turning Point* (New York, 1965). Useful memoirs include those of Socialist Revolutionary leader Victor M. Chernov, *The Great Russian Revolution*, trans. Philip E. Mosely (New Haven, Conn., 1936) and those of two Menshevik participants and observers, N. N. Sukhanov, *The Russian Revolution 1917*, ed. and trans. Joel Carmichael (2 vols., New York, 1962) and W. S. Woytinsky, *Stormy Passage* (New York, 1961).

Excellent analyses of the political parties involved include the two books by Rabinowitch cited above; Oliver H. Radkey, *The Agrarian Foes of Bolshevism* (New York, 1958), which treats the Socialist Revolutionaries; and William G. Rosenberg, *Liberals in the Russian Revolution: The Constitutional Democratic Party, 1917–1921* (Princeton, N. J., 1974). See also the pertinent chapters in Paul Avrich, *The Russian Anarchists* (Princeton, N. J., 1967).

Specific issues in the revolution are treated in Graeme J. Gill, *Peasants and Government in the Russian Revolution* (New York, 1979); Richard Pipes, *The Formation of the Soviet Union** (rev. ed., New York, 1968); Robert D. Warth, *The Allies and the Russian Revolution* (Durham, N. C. 1954); Rex A. Wade, *The Russian Search for Peace, February–October, 1917* (Stanford, Calif., 1969); and Richard K. Debo, *Revolution and Survival: The Foreign Policy of Soviet Russia, 1917–1918* (Toronto, 1979).

First-hand accounts and impressions are collected in Dimitri von Mohrenschildt (ed.), *The Russian Revolution of 1917: Contemporary*

---

* Available in paperback.

Accounts (New York, 1971) and Roger Pethybridge (ed.), *Witnesses to the Russian Revolution* (London, 1964).

Two fine historical novels that reveal much about the motives and passions that fueled the revolution are Boris Pasternak, *Dr. Zhivago* (New York, 1958) and two volumes by Mikhail Sholokhov, *And Quiet Flows the Don** and *The Don Flows Home to the Sea,** trans. Stephen Garry (New York, 1964 and 1969).

An excellent collection of photographs and art from the revolutionary period is Harrison E. Salisbury, *Russia in Revolution, 1900–1930** (New York, 1978).

* Available in paperback.

Chronology of the Russian Revolution of 1917

★

All dates are given according to the modern Gregorian calendar, which was thirteen days ahead of the calendar used in Russia in 1917.

1917

March 8   International Women's Day celebrated in Petrograd. Crowds on streets. Lines at bread stores.

March 9   Many workers on strike or locked out of factories by management. Street crowds grow.

March 10   Strikes spread. Several hundred thousand involved. First clashes with police and shooting.

March 11   Tsar Nicholas II dissolves Duma and orders disturbances suppressed. Firing on demonstrators, with some casualties.

March 12   Several units of garrison troops mutiny; soldiers mingle with street crowds. Petrograd Soviet of Workers' Deputies organized. Duma leaders form temporary committee.

Appendix

March 13   Authorities in Petrograd stop trying to prevent revolution. Duma leaders begin talks with Soviet leaders concerning establishment of new government. Tsarist ministers arrested.

March 14   Petrograd Soviet issues Order No. 1 on army conditions. Soldiers' section added to Soviet.

March 15   Nicholas II abdicates in favor of brother, Grand Duke Michael, who next day rejects throne. Temporary committee of Duma forms Provisional government.

March 27   Petrograd Soviet calls for peace "without annexations or indemnities."

April 16   Lenin arrives in Petrograd from exile in Switzerland.

April 20   Lenin's "April Theses" published, urging Bolshevik party to take more radical stance.

May 3   Publication of note from Foreign Minister Miliukov to Allies reaffirming patriotic war aims. Street demonstrations erupt in protest. First governmental crisis begins.

May 15   Miliukov resigns.

May 17   Trotsky reaches Petrograd from exile in United States.

May 18   First coalition cabinet of Provisional government formed, including socialist ministers and Kerensky as minister of war.

June 16–   Meetings of First All-Russian Congress of Soviets.
July 17

June 29   Provisional government orders major offensive against Austro-Hungarian and German armies.

July 1   Soviet-sponsored mass demonstration in Petrograd dominated by Bolshevik slogans and groups.

July 15   Kadet ministers resign over policy toward Ukraine; second governmental crisis begins.

July 16–18   Mass demonstrations and street disturbances known as "July Days." Followed by repressive measures against Bolsheviks.

July 19	Russian offensive fails; German counteroffensive begins.
July 29	General Kornilov named commander-in-chief of army.
Aug. 5	Trotsky and other Bolsheviks arrested; Lenin in hiding.
Aug. 6	Second coalition cabinet formed, with Kerensky as prime minister.
Aug. 25–28	State Conference in Moscow meets; strikes in protest in Moscow.
Sept. 9–12	Abortive counterrevolutionary movement led by General Kornilov.
Sept. 14–22	Lenin, still in hiding, writes urging moderate course for Bolsheviks.
Sept. 17	Trotsky freed on bail.
Sept. 22	Bolsheviks win control of Petrograd Soviet.
Sept. 25–27	Lenin changes his mind, calls for radical policy.
Sept. 27–Oct. 4	Democratic Conference meets and elects "Pre-Parliament."
Oct. 2	Bolsheviks win control of Moscow Soviet.
Oct. 7	Third coalition cabinet formed.
Oct. 20	Pre-Parliament convenes; Bolsheviks walk out.
Oct. 22	Petrograd Soviet votes to set up Military Revolutionary Committee.
Oct. 23	At Lenin's urging Bolshevik Central Committee votes "armed insurrection the order of the day."
Oct. 29–30	Despite opposition of Zinoviev and Kamenev, Bolshevik Central Committee reaffirms previous vote and authorizes preparations for armed uprising.
Oct. 30	Opposition of Zinoviev and Kamenev to Bolshevik plans made public in newspapers.
Nov. 4	Government loses control of garrison troops when representatives of military units agree only orders

confirmed by Military Revolutionary Committee will be obeyed.

Nov. 5   Military Revolutionary Committee wins over forces of Peter and Paul Fortress.

Nov. 6   Provisional government moves against Military Revolutionary Committee and Bolshevik press; orders transfer of loyal troops to Petrograd. Kerensky's appeal to Pre-Parliament rebuffed.

Nov. 7   During early morning hours units linked to Military Revolutionary Committee occupy key points, including post office, telegraph offices, train stations. Midmorning Kerensky leaves Petrograd by car to seek loyal forces at front. Forces of Military Revolutionary Committee close Pre-Parliament at noon. By evening Winter Palace under seige by antigovernment units. At 11:00 P.M. the Second All-Russian Congress of Soviets convenes.

Nov. 8   Pro-Soviet forces occupy Winter Palace shortly after midnight; arrest ministers of Provisional Government. Congress of Soviets passes Leninist decrees on peace and on land; forms new government—Council of People's Commissars—composed of Bolsheviks, headed by Lenin.

Nov. 9–15   Struggle in Moscow between forces loyal to Provisional government and those of Bolshevik-led Moscow Soviet; latter triumphs.

Nov. 14   Kerensky's march on Petrograd with troops loyal to him collapses; Kerensky flees.

Nov. 25–27 Elections to Constituent Assembly; Socialist Revolutionaries win majority.

Dec. 3   Soviet appointee assumes command of army.

Dec. 15   Armistice between Russia and Germany and Austria-Hungary.

Dec. 22   Left Socialist Revolutionaries agree to enter Soviet government.

1918

Jan. 18–19   Constituent Assembly convenes, then dispersed by Soviet forces.

March 3   Soviet government signs Treaty of Brest-Litovsk with Germany.

Index

199

DATE DUE